GROUND OF THE HEART

GROUND OF THE HEART

A Commentary on
the General Thanksgiving

BY W. W. S. MARCH
Vicar of Eastbourne
Prebendary of Chichester

FOREWORD BY

THE ARCHBISHOP OF CANTERBURY

Give thanks, O Israel, unto God the Lord
in the congregations:
From the ground of the heart
Psalm 68 : 26, Prayer Book Version

THE FAITH PRESS
7 TUFTON STREET LONDON S.W. 1
MOREHOUSE-BARLOW CO. INC. NEW YORK U.S.A.

FIRST PUBLISHED IN 1963

241.36
M331

PRINTED IN GREAT BRITAIN
in 10pt. Baskerville type
BY THE FAITH PRESS LTD
LEIGHTON BUZZARD

FOREWORD

BY THE ARCHBISHOP OF CANTERBURY

HOWEVER many are the requests for the revision or modernizing of our forms of service the General Thanksgiving retains its hold upon the affection of those who join in public worship. Both the trained churchgoer and the casual attender find in its words and cadences something which goes home to their thought and feeling. There are reasons for this. One is that thanksgiving is an ineradicable instinct, and another is that the words of this form convey deep theology with the simplicity which depth alone affords.

This book, like the General Thanksgiving which it expounds, goes deep into theology and at the same time speaks simply to any man or woman who knows what it is to be grateful and that it is to God that gratitude is due. It shows us how thanksgiving goes to the ground of our being and discloses our relation to the Creator and the created world. No less helpful is the treatment of the bearing of thanksgiving upon the experience of joy and pain in our lives. We are shown how thanksgiving in the midst of painful circumstances has been able to transform both the circumstances and the people who experience them.

I know of no other book that does what this book does, and it will cause many readers to be grateful for what it does. It expounds the words of a great prayer in their historical context in the seventeenth century, in their theological depth and in their power to express the needs and aspirations of human souls to-day. It will help many to a 'due sense of God's mercies,' to a more faithful use of 'the means of grace' and to a surer grasp of 'the hope of glory.'

MICHAEL CANTUAR:

ALMIGHTY GOD, Father of all mercies,
We thine unworthy servants
    do give thee most humble and hearty thanks
For all thy goodness and loving-kindness
To us and to all men;

We bless thee for our creation, preservation,
    and all the blessings of this life;
But above all, for thine inestimable love
In the redemption of the world by our Lord
    Jesus Christ,
For the means of grace,
And for the hope of glory.

And, we beseech thee,
    give us that due sense of all thy mercies,
That our hearts may be unfeignedly thankful,
And that we shew forth thy praise,
Not only with our lips, but in our lives;
By giving up ourselves to thy service,
And by walking before thee
    in holiness and righteousness all our days;
    through Jesus Christ our Lord,
    to whom with thee and the Holy Ghost
    be all honour and glory
    world without end.
    AMEN

PREFACE

When in the parable the younger son at last returned home, he found his father running out to meet him. Very probably he burst into tears. He was also deeply thankful.

That combination of sorrow with thankfulness is a symbol of Christian experience. To be human is to be immersed in sorrow of every sort: repentance and regrets, agonies and pains, bereavement, frustration, failure, and—typical of the present century—anxieties. To be a Christian is at the same time to be returning home, and therefore to be thankful.

Our *General Thanksgiving* challenges us to come to terms with this interior tension in our lives. It is therefore not unsuitable for use at a time of self-training such as Lent. When the festival fanfares are silent and the soul is centred on themes of dust and ashes a Christian's thanksgiving can be seen for what it is: not varnish put on what is pleasant in a vain attempt at preservation, but a thread woven into the stuff of real life, which includes suffering and storms and death.

Christ endured the Cross for the joy that was set before him. We share his joy long before we get to our crosses, and our aim as Christians is to see that the joy shall remain, as he promised, throughout our Gethsemanes and lesser Crucifixions, because we already have his Easter.

This can happen when we faithfully follow the pattern of this prayer and let our thanksgivings be prompted by the deep facts of our religion. Those who thank God fitfully and in the sunshine may give thanks on the surface, but those who thank him for his acts of love thank him on dark days also and 'from the ground of the heart.'

CONTENTS

CHAPTER 1

BEGINNINGS OF THANKS

1

At first sight thanksgiving is absent from much of the New Testament. There is no mention of it in the Sermon on the Mount; neither the Beatitudes nor the Lord's Prayer speak of it. Only one of the parables of Jesus refers to it, and then as a warning against its misuse by the Pharisee. In the accounts of the healing miracles there is a similar and surprising silence; again only once is thankfulness alluded to—on the occasion of the cure of the ten lepers—and here it is interwoven with other themes in the tale and plays a subordinate role. The most famous passages in St. Paul's letters appear to give it no greater prominence. Thanksgiving is not listed among the pieces of the armour of God, the three great virtues of 1 Corinthians 13, or the nine fruits of the Spirit. The Christian scriptures, which indisputably set the pattern of experience in the Christian life, are occupied with a vast portrayal of the love and justice of God and a rich range of human response; yet repeatedly they give nothing more than hints of a thanksgiving which that response if genuine must undoubtedly contain.

But there are other contexts in the New Testament in which thanksgiving not only is mentioned, but also becomes the decisive and dominant mood both of writer and readers. It is significant that these passages occur in the epistles. The letters which the first Christians exchanged and circulated are first-hand evidence of the outlook and personal faith in the light of which the gospel narratives were selected, for the sake of which they were preserved.

Ground of the Heart

According to the New English Bible these master statements of our theme are:

'in the name of our Lord Jesus Christ give thanks everyday for everything to our God and Father' (Ephes. 5 : 20);

'in everything make your requests known to God in prayer and petition with thanksgiving' (Phil. 4 : 6);

'let your hearts overflow with thankfulness' (Col. 2 : 7);

'give thanks whatever happens' (1 Thess. 5 : 18).

This evidence is in a class of its own. The statements do not depend for their importance upon their number; what is outstanding about them is their quality. They do not need to be repeated. They describe a thanksgiving which is continuous. A thanksgiving like that has only to be mentioned once for it to be recognized as always at hand.

This continuous thanksgiving is built on the foundation of God's continuous love. Whether the divine action is recognized in the mystery of creation or in the self-disclosing revelation of redemption, that action according to the New Testament writers is the spur to an expectant gratitude which, while receiving and acknowledging spiritual mercies, is always ready to receive more. Romans 8, centred on verse 28, is the Christian's charter for this: in the familiar Authorized Version, 'we know that all things work together for good to them that love God, to them who are called according to his purpose'; in the New English Bible, 'in everything, as we know, he co-operates for good with those who love God and are called according to his purpose.' This startlingly vivid presentation of an attitude which can joyfully rely on the purposes of God roundly defeats any attempt to maintain that thanksgiving has no place in the pages of the New Testament. Its theme is that of a thanksgiving which in a Christian's life is not only uninterrupted, but uninterruptible. It cannot be torn into shreds and tatters by argument, doubt or misfortune. It cannot be sliced any more than a stream can. This thanksgiving flows and overflows so that a thousand statements of its nature or characteristics could not exhaust it, and the alleged silences of scripture with regard to it have the appearance of being the surfaces of a single unfathomed deep.

It cannot be said that thanksgiving of this type is encouraged by the Book of Common Prayer. If it be the function of a Christian liturgy to bring to the surface the hidden spiritual treasures of the scriptures and to give voice to the inarticulate yearnings of a worshipping community, the English liturgy cannot in this respect be described as an unqualified success. Thanksgivings occur in the Prayer Book, but they tend to crop up as incidental items during forms of worship which are acts of penitence or of petition. In the order for the Holy Communion the eucharistic note is present, but muted. In the daily offices psalms of praise and canticles take their place as secondary elements in the cycle of worship. The twentieth century worshipper has to rely on specific 'Services of Thanksgiving' for any adequate expression of his thanks after some national or private emergency. Failing these he must fall back on the vicar's limited repertoire of favourite hymns, which has become the typically contemporary method of transforming a set service of intercession or sorrow for sin into an offering of praise.

The deficiency has not gone unnoticed. The Lambeth Conference of 1958 appealed for the more extensive provision of litanies, of thanksgiving and adoration, as well as of intercession, and pleaded for a strengthening of the mood of thanksgiving by making eucharistic worship more explicitly a commemoration of the resurrection, ascension and glorification of our Lord.

A century earlier observations, not incompatible with these recommendations, were being made from the side of the Tractarians. The writer of Number 86 of *Tracts for the Times* concluded from his scrutiny of the collects and other portions of the Prayer Book that the translators and compilers made changes which definitely reduced the note of confidence or joy. The Collect of Trinity XX survives as an exception in employing the word 'cheerfully' as an indication of the manner in which Christians desire to accomplish those things which God would have them do, although even here there is a hint of mere resignation.

We can trace this uneasiness about the scarcity of references to gladness in religion to the generations who were themselves trying out the earlier versions of the English Prayer Book.

During the formative years in which our Prayer Book was under revision one prayer took shape which was to illuminate the rest.

This composition could not at one stroke change the colour of the entire liturgy for it was only one among many prayers. But it went some way towards making amends for the obvious neglect of thanksgiving which had so far persisted, and still persists, in English forms of worship. To the remarkable career and character of this prayer we now turn.

2

The prayer called *A General Thanksgiving* came into the Book of Common Prayer as part of the additions which were incorporated by the Savoy Conference in 1661. It was composed by Edward Reynolds, who became Bishop of Norwich in that year.

Both the date and the authorship have a bearing on the significance of the prayer.

The year 1661 marked what was hoped would be the end of a long and wearing time of changes and upheavals in worship and in daily life. To say that this time of flux had begun in 1549 is an understatement. Changes of such great import have their beginnings in unrecorded ideas and decisions of a people and of their spokesmen. But taking that date as marking a stage in the process and visualizing what would be involved in a parallel in our own times by a period of equal uncertainties from 1849 to 1961, still our assessment would not only comprise that definite stretch of time but a series of events which were of overwhelming intensity and violence for the land. The disturbances before and after the Elizabethan Settlement, the martyrdoms on either side, the Civil War, the death on the scaffold of Charles I, the Commonwealth under Oliver Cromwell and after him, were all preliminaries to the decisive days of the restoration of the monarchy in the person of Charles II in 1660.

The Savoy Conference which was to provide the new Book of Common Prayer met in the following year, and then relief was in the air. To some extent both puritan and anglican shared this mood. Men now had the paramount desire to give thanks to the Lord, even though not all might agree on what they were giving thanks for; and the man chosen to put into words this great upsurge of feeling was well equipped by experience and temperament.

Edward Reynolds was born in 1599 and died in 1676; which meant that his life spanned the period of commotions. As a young man he became chaplain to the King and an incumbent in Northampton, but this did not prevent him from holding office during the Commonwealth as vicar of St. Lawrence Jewry and Dean of Christ Church, Oxford. At the Restoration he was again accepted as an anglican, and at once set to work to reconcile the opposing sides. In providing the *General Thanksgiving* for the new Prayer Book he was in fact undertaking the task of producing a prayer which would ring true in the worship of as many of his contemporaries as possible, incorporating material from a variety of sources, making use of words and phrases which were already familiar to adherents of both the main movements. His purpose was to enable all worshippers to feel at home when the new *Thanksgiving* was said.

The composition of this prayer was the achievement of a reconciler. But more, it testified to the survival, in the midst of the most inhospitable surroundings, of the spirit of thankfulness. Reynolds made full use of prayers which were already in circulation, drawing on Edward VI's *Primer*; a thanks-giving attached to the Elizabethan Homilies of 1562; a prayer by Cranmer; another by Harry Becon, Cranmer's chaplain. The nearest parallel to the language of *A General Thanks-giving* is the opening to a thanksgiving said to have been composed by Queen Elizabeth I herself after one of her royal progresses: 'I render unto thee, O merciful and heavenly Father, most humble and hearty thanks for thy manifold mercies so abundantly bestowed upon me, as well for my creation, preservation, regeneration, and all other thy bene-fits and great mercies exhibited in Christ Jesus.' The supply of such examples shows that there was no lack of material available to Bishop Reynolds. His expressions were largely derived from these earlier prayers. But it was their survival, no less than their derivation, which counted. These proved that even during the upheavals and terrors through which his generation had passed the deep spirit of Christian thankful-ness had not been quenched. 'We live in failing times,' Rey-nolds had declaimed in his sermon, 'The Brand Plucked from the Fire,' which he preached before the Lord Mayor of London at St. Paul's on November 5th, 1659, 'We live in failing times. We have found men of low degree vanity, and men of high degree a lie. We have leaned on our house, but it did not stand; we have leaned on our staff, and it hath gone into our hand. . . . Our ships have been broken, our trade broken, our estates broken, our government broken, our hopes broken, our Church broken; nothing but our hearts and our sins unbroken. A sad thing, that a people will be quite fatherless, before they will think of going to God.' This tale of woe might with very few alterations become the lament of any prophet who in writing or speaking feels an urge to expose the failure of religion and the consequent moral degeneracy in his time. The remarkable fact is that it is the description of the days which preserved and handed on thanksgivings; and it was written and delivered by the man who was to gather up those thanksgivings and cast them in the form in which they have now been used for three hundred years.

3

The circumstances in which our *General Thanksgiving* came to be written give prominence to the outstanding feature of all Christian gratitude to God. The prayer could in no sense be claimed to be a mirror of its environment. It does not put forward thankfulness as in any respect a product of its age. This feature is constant in Christian experience. Expression of a Christian's thankfulness is not dependent on outward conditions or material considerations. It does not involve a gratitude which is chained to ease or luxury, to prosperity or even peace. It will not pin a man to earth, but rather uplift him. It points heavenward. Therefore an age where anarchy threatens and security is at stake can be a setting for the clearest and most brilliant exposition of it. Even when 'the blessings of this life' seem to be few, the Christian's gratitude remains unbounded; for it ranges over the blessings which speak of another life. It ties us to eternity.

This fact turns the *General Thanksgiving* into a typically twentieth century prayer. Thankfulness will not flourish amongst contemporary men if it is supposed to be a product of our own times. Once it is perceived as an addition, a contribution, or as some might say an injection, which the Christian derives from some other world and in turn passes on to his environment and his fellows, it can be recognized and welcomed as a real and lasting attitude. Thankfulness involves response on man's part. This is in part response to the world. But it is not response to a world in isolation from God. The response in the last resort is to God himself, and those conditions in the world which attack the buoyancy of human optimism can never be equivalent to cancellations of true thankfulness. In the life of faith the most adverse circumstances are the opportunities for thanksgiving.

Our own century is in obvious respects a large-scale replica of much that was familiar to the writer of this prayer. We have our disorders and anxieties, multiplied and magnified. These can no more be mirrored by a pose of thankfulness now than in the previous age. The modern situation endorses with a characteristically sharp touch a truth which the Christian knows to be relevant to the environment of man in any generation. He is prepared to give thanks for material benefits which at any moment are granted him, but he knows that the inner spring of his thankfulness is spiritual. In training himself to be a thankful person he is taking in his stride the passing show. His disciplined thanks are built on that which lasts. Therefore the spiritual blessings which are unaffected by 'the changes and chances of this mortal life' are the ultimate reasons for his 'humble and hearty thanks,' and these are what have ensured for our prayer its unquestioned popularity.

This prayer met the needs of men from the moment when it was written. It has not failed them since. This is made clear by the way in which it has been transformed. When Bishop Reynolds wrote it, the *Thanksgiving* was intended to be said as a collect type of prayer by the minister alone. In the 1662 Book there were no directions for the congregation to join in vocally, save in the Amen which was printed in italics to indicate this. No capital letters were printed to mark the beginnings of clauses where a pause might be made in corporate use, as in the General Confession at Morning or Evening Prayer, or at the Communion. Further, as if to render it impossible for the congregation to say this prayer with the minister, there was the clause in parenthesis, corresponding to a similar provision in the parallel Prayer for All Sorts and Conditions of Men, giving an opportunity for reference to special mercies : 'particularly to those who desire now to offer up their praises and thanksgivings for thy late mercies vouchsafed unto them.'

But the people have made this prayer their own. In defiance of the rubric and without any official direction they have themselves turned it into a prayer which they regularly say with the minister. The pressure has undoubtedly come from the pew rather than from the reading desk, and the 1928 Prayer Book gave in to it. Accordingly the Revised Prayer Book has introduced capitals to denote the main clauses. As a compromise a direction in the form of a new rubric has been introduced, describing the prayer as 'A general Thanksgiving to be said by the Minister alone, or by the Minister and people.' The ambiguity here cannot be said to be satisfactory. It is underlined by the retention of the parenthesis 'to be said when any that have been prayed for desire to return praise,' although this could not be used in a prayer which minister and people say together; and a footnote is added to that effect. But in practice the ambiguity of the rubric has been swept aside, again by the people. Only on very rare occasions—and then in such places as a College Chapel or Cathedral—is this prayer now said 'by the Minister alone.' Our congregations have claimed it as their own. It is one of the few examples of prayers in which the modern Christian congregation expects to join, saying it with the minister, and it is now one of the main prayers which Christian congregations who are not anglican also willingly use. In its life of three hundred years this *Thanksgiving* has been transformed from a collect to be said alone by the minister of one particular denomination into a congregational act of worship which, like its author, has an ecumenical outlook. Compiled within the Church of England, it is now available and acceptable far beyond her borders.

But this transformation is not the result of the choices of one generation or of the circumstances of one time. We are to see that *A General Thanksgiving* reflects neither the joys nor the distresses of any one century. It is the expression of a timeless cry from the heart of man. It is applicable to men of all centuries, for its central focus is on God.

CHAPTER 2

THANKS, PRAISE AND WONDER

1

'This poor word.' So Evelyn Underhill (1875–1941) described thanksgiving when considering it as the English equivalent of 'eucharist.' The 'suggestion of dutiful gratitude for benefits received,' which undoubtedly is associated in most modern minds with the word, is the reason for its poverty. According to her, thanksgiving in its Christian context should include all that the term has embraced from the very beginning of its use in the early Church as 'eucharist.' Evelyn Underhill's complaint was that the English word 'is far from suggesting that total adoring acknowledgement of God in his cosmic splendour and merciful dealings with men, that disinterested worship, that delighted Godward reference and consequent sanctifying action, which this word implied first for devout Jews, and then for those early Christians who so promptly adopted it as the best of all titles for their chief religious rite.' [1]

The richness of this word, when interpreted as denoting responsive attitudes to God in addition to what we ordinarily mean by gratefulness, need not in the first place have been restricted to that central rite, although in the pattern of Christian worship it came to be centred on it. The same author points out that in a sense 'eucharistic action' runs through the whole range of a Christian's life. Once a human being turns in faith to his maker he knows himself to be a creature, able by reason and affection to approach his Creator. That immediately places him in the eucharistic mood. His whole approach to God is to be 'covered, directed, and

[1] E. Underhill, *Worship,* 1936, p. 141.

coloured by thanksgiving.' The approach itself, the entry into the divine presence, 'is all occasioned and made possible first by his gracious movement towards us, and then by the incitements of his grace.' This inner movement of worshipful response to God springs from our status as creatures and our desire to return to the Creator. Miss Underhill quotes as 'perhaps the chief source of the great eucharistic prayers of the early Church the dramatic statement of the heavenly adoration given in Revelation 4 : 11' (our version is from the New English Bible).

'Thou art worthy, O Lord our God, to receive glory and honour and power, because thou didst create all things; by thy will they were created, and have their being!'

This insight into the richness of what a Christian can mean by thanksgiving is denied to most anglican worshippers on account of a noticeable omission in their liturgy.

In the Holy Communion service as provided by the Book of Common Prayer thanksgiving concentrates on the work of Christ in redemption to the exclusion of the work of the Father in creation. In the Sursum Corda and the Preface thanks are offered, and the people are summoned to join in the offering. But there is scarcely any mention of occasions for thanksgiving outside the mysteries of the life of Christ; and this impression is confirmed by the set of Proper Prefaces which reasonably lay all their stress upon the redemptive significance of particular festivals. This means that the notes of adoration and thanksgiving are not entirely absent. Indeed when these are strengthened by the addition of anthem or hymn at a sung Communion Service the worshipper cannot remain in doubt as to these strains in his worship being powerful elements in the eucharistic action. But these glad notes refer to redemption, and not creation. In the primitive Christian liturgies there was no such dichotomy. Both Creation and Redemption were recalled as the grounds for

21

'eucharist.' Sometimes the act of remembrance was made in language which to modern Western ears would sound over elaborate and exuberant. But by way of reaction we find that we have inherited an opposite extreme. The austerity of our English rite, though demanded at a time when excesses needed to be curbed, deprives the majority of our worshippers of this rich insight into the nature of thanksgiving which we now only reach after additional thought or instruction. The bread and wine are called 'creatures'; in addition the worshippers must know themselves to be creatures; then the eucharist begins to be recognizable as an act of worship addressed to the Creator.

When the attention of the communicant is thus directed to both Creation and Redemption, and not to either exclusive of the other, the fuller implications of his thanks to God become apparent and the whole of his discipleship can become 'eucharistic.' In giving thanks to God he is doing far more than saying a dutiful 'Thank you' to a dutifully generous and bountiful heavenly Parent. The gratitude is there. But it is taken up into the majestic sweep of wonder, awe, and acknowledgment of divine might. Creaturely dependence is seen to consist not in a series of occasions, when, corresponding to crises and emergencies in our lives we receive doles or gratuities from on high, but in a perpetual condition of abasement, helplessness and—because of the divine mercies—of joy. Far more than gratitude is involved. But it is all named thanksgiving, it is all 'eucharist.'

We shall return later to the intimate relationship between the Christian's thanksgiving—including that expression of it which we now name *A General Thanksgiving*—and the eucharist, or in other words between the life-eucharist of a Christian and his eucharistic worship. Our concern now is the recovery of the wider meanings which the word thanksgiving itself can carry.

First we may notice the bearing on our *General Thanksgiving* of the familiar distinction between thanks and praise. The distinction is a common-place of present day instruction and discipleship. Beginners in prayer are encouraged to preserve it, and systematic doctrine makes use of it. According to this distinction we thank God for his gifts : we praise him for Who he is. And the suggestion which is implied is that praise is considerably superior to thanks. Praise is evoked by consideration of the actions of God as well as of his nature. Clearly, gifts received are less than either his acts or his being. Hence, it is supposed, thanks are less than praise, and the Christian who is willing to grow in his faith is urged to progress beyond his thanks to praise.

The distinction has become stereotyped as a result of conventional phrases in Christian worship which give the impression that the two words stand for two distinct experiences in the spiritual life. For example, very few of the psalms are exhortations to thank the Lord : a great number call the worshipper to praise him. But this may be largely accounted for as an accident of translation. It is open to question whether or no the mind of the Prayer Book really is that thanks and praise are two different methods of approach to God, and that praise is superior. 'Whoso offereth me thanks and praise, he honoureth me' (Ps. 50 : 23),—the anglican is expected to repeat on the tenth morning of the month. What he is not likely to know is that this translation of the verse amongst those which are current to-day is peculiar to the Prayer Book and that the rest of the main English versions omit the distinction and put only one of the two : either 'praise' (A.V.) or 'thanks' (Moffat) or 'thanksgiving' (R.V. and R.S.V.).

What is certain is that the *General Thanksgiving* does not observe a rigid distinction between the two. In the opening of the prayer we give 'most humble and hearty thanks' : in the conclusion we ask that we may be 'unfeignedly thankful' and 'shew forth' God's 'praise.' Again, the rubric at the side of the prayer draws attention to the italicized sentence 'to be said when any that have been prayed for desire to return, (not thanksgiving, but) praise,' while the sentence itself refers to those who 'desire now to offer up their praises and thanksgivings.' Lastly, in the body of the prayer there is a repeated stress on 'blessings of this life,' 'thine inestimable love,' 'mercies,' but no express mention of gifts. We are driven to conclude that the writer of this prayer did not wish to press home our distinction. He is making no clear-cut division between the nature of God and the gifts of God. The mood of analysis is not the mood of this *Thanksgiving*. According to it thanks and praise are not to be precisely distinguished. The one shades into the other, or rather the one illuminates the other. Although at any one time or in any particular century the two words might develop their particular significance, they are in fact closely interconnected, and a Christian loses the richness in the meanings of both if he attempts in the interest of accuracy to separate them. If praise, together with all the unspoken acts of adoring love which are associated with praise, be stripped from thanksgiving, a simple gratitude may remain, but little else; and conversely it is difficult to conceive how the soul as creature will experience gratitude to the Creator without leaping forward in worship to love and adore. Thus, Christian thanksgiving, through its kinship with praise, is invested with an eternal quality. Of praise the Victorian evangelical, Bishop J. C. Ryle (1816–1910), wrote that 'it is the only part of our worship which will never die. Preaching, praying and reading will one day be no longer needed. But praise will continue throughout eternity.' [2] We may say the same of thanksgiving.

The close affinity between thanks and praise was accepted without question by the author of our *Thanksgiving*, as his own writings testify. A significant example is the passage in

[2] J. C. Ryle, *Thoughts on Public Worship*, 1960, p. 10. Reprinted from *Principles of Churchmen*, 1884.

which Bishop Reynolds, while expounding the ability and the duty of man to make some return for the 'mercies' which he receives, makes no reference to 'thanks' but speaks only of 'praises.'

> There is no such rich return from earth to Heaven as praise : this is indeed the only tribute we can pay unto God,—to value and celebrate his goodness towards us. As, in the flux and reflux of the sea, the water that in the one comes from the sea into the shore, doth, in the other, but run back into itself again ; so praises are, as it were, the return of mercies into themselves, or into that home and fountain of God's love whence they flowed.

According to God's ordering 'the creatures among themselves' enjoy 'a kind of natural confederacy . . . each one receiving and returning, deriving unto others, and drawing from others what serves most for the conservation of them all,' and this arrangement within the created order is a means by which God teaches 'the souls of men to maintain the like spiritual commerce and confederacy with Heaven, to have all the passages between them and it open and unobstructed,—that the mercies which they receive from thence may not be kept under and imprisoned in unthankfulness, but may have a free way in daily praises, to return to their fountain again.'[3] In this exposition Reynolds has moved rapidly from one metaphor to another, first thinking in terms of the tide, next in terms of commerce, lastly in terms of imprisonment and release from prison. But his thought is clear throughout this compact argument. If mercies are not to be met by unthankfulness, praises—he does not mention thanks—are to be offered, and these praises are the richest returns which we can possibly make in our response as creatures to God.

Reynolds repeated this point, stressing it as a portrayal of an essential element in the Christian's life, and indeed in the

[3] *Works*, Vol. III, pp. 245-6.

Church's life. Preaching from Psalm 147, verses 12–15, before the Lord Mayor of London on the day of Thanksgiving for God's 'long and gracious preservation of that great city, from Pestilence, Fire, and other Dangers' he had his supreme opportunity of developing the theme.

> The Lord, having shewed mercies unto the Church, requireth that they be not buried in oblivion, but that the glory and praise of them be acknowledged unto him. Great luminaries have certain beams, as pipes and channels, through which their light is derived and diffused upon others. Thanksgiving is the beam of an enlightened soul, whereby it maketh report of those mercies, which, from the Father of light, hath been shed abroad upon it. Every thing naturally returns to its original. 'All rivers run into the sea ; unto the place from whence they come, thither they return to go.' (Eccles. 1 : 7.) A straight line drawn into length, the further it goes, is still the weaker ; but in a circle, returning to its first point and original, it recovers strength : so the creature, the further it goes from God, is still the weaker, till it return back to him again. And the best way of returning into him, is by praising him : for praises are the language of heaven, where it is that men are perfectly taken home to God.[4]

In this exuberant and enthusiastic manner the writer of our *Thanksgiving* could describe the nature and necessity of thanks as praise or of praise as thanks. And throughout he would hold to the point that the praise which is offered by man to God is a return, and only a return. Always praise is a creaturely activity ; and in relation to God it can add nothing to the receiver. 'Nothing is hereby added unto him, but only his own glory acknowledged and adored by the Church ; as when the sun shines on a diamond, the lustre thereof is not increased, but reported.'[5]

[4] *Works,* Vol. V, p. 5.
[5] Ibid.

It follows that although we speak of giving praise to God, we can only use the word 'giving' in a special, almost metaphorical, sense. We give, but do not 'increase' any property or attribute of God : we solely 'report' his love and glory, and that is all that our giving of praise to him can do. To quote Bishop Reynolds again, 'God is all-sufficient unto himself, and standeth not in need of any of his creatures to add any excellence unto him, any more than the sun doth of the light of a candle.' [6] And later, 'Not therefore for any advantage or accession unto himself (who cannot be a gainer by his creatures) but only for our benefit and comfort, is the Lord pleased to require praises for his people : as the window admitteth the light of the sun, not for the benefit of the sun, but of the house into which it shineth.' [7]

3

By keeping thanks and praise together the *General Thanksgiving* is emphasizing a basic fact in the interior life of a Christian. Christian thanksgiving is not to be preserved or practised in isolation. The impoverishment of the word, of which Miss Underhill complained, occurs when that is attempted. It belongs to a family of words, all of which share the family likeness of an adoring, humble, creaturely and abased approach to God.

The Eucharist gives two examples of these words coming together in one group. First, at the *Sursum Corda* the call, 'Let us give thanks unto our Lord God,' is followed by :

It is very meet, right, and our bounden duty, that we should at all times, and in all places, give thanks unto thee, O Lord. . . . Therefore . . . we laud and magnify thy glorious name ; evermore praising thee, and saying, Holy, holy, holy . . .

[6] *Works,* Vol. V, p. 4.
[7] Ibid., p. 6.

Here 'thanks,' 'laud,' 'magnify,' 'praise,' swiftly follow one another in one unbroken surge of worship.

Secondly, the 'Glory be to God on high' includes a similar sequence in its opening paragraph.

> We praise thee, we bless thee, we worship thee, we glorify thee, we give thanks to thee for thy great glory.

This example is particularly remarkable, for 'thanks' now appears in the place of 'praise' as the culmination of the series, and 'thanks' is here offered not for gifts, nor for blessings, nor for the hope of our own glory, but for God's 'great glory.' This is to imply that the Christian's use of thanksgiving no less than his praise can, and at times does, refer to God's being, his nature, Who he is.

Too careful a distinction between these words of worship leads to error. It is in worship that they are used; and worship by its very nature brings our small, precise minds into touch with the transcendent wonders of the Divine Being. We are speaking of the fringes of that territory in human experience where boundaries cannot be defined; and if we find ourselves advancing inside that land of wonder from one type of country-side to another, then we do well to give up attempting to trace where the change of scene has occurred and to let our attention dwell solely upon the new joys which are encountered. Another metaphor is of help. We may compare the different rich strands in worship, indicated by words like 'thanks,' 'praise,' 'honour,' 'glorify,' to the varying colours in a rainbow. The plain appreciative observer notices the different colours, although he cannot tell at which exact point one colour ceases and another begins. It is sufficient, and more than sufficient, for him that he can echo:

> My heart leaps up when I behold
> A rainbow in the sky.

There may be special features of worship which are similarly stressed in either 'glorify' or 'magnify' or 'praise' or 'thank.'

But far from it being the case that we can recognize at which point each of these may run into one or more of the others, the growth of a Christian in his worship suggests that his advance will reveal to him that ultimately all coalesce into one and that our distinctions between them, used and accepted in this life, are, in the literal sense, but temporary. At the end all these strands will be indistinguishably blended. Their present distinctness is an accommodation to our present limited perceptions.

While therefore we are bound to consider thanksgiving, as we might also examine intercession or confession or petition, as though it were a department of prayer or worship which could be put into practice on its own, we have constantly to see it as a strand in a single, but complex and interwoven, act of worship. For the purpose of enquiry or understanding it is essential to make the distinction; but in the living process of worship the distinction is subsidiary to the total offering of the soul. It will be no less justifiable to speak of giving thanks for what God gives than for Who he is, or of praising him for either. The humble, worshipping Christian need not worry to find out whether he is actually giving praise or giving thanks. What is vital is that he knows himself to be making the act of self-offering and abasement which in its different aspects can be described as both and more.

It follows that, although our reflections on the *Thanksgiving* will naturally include a catalogue of the causes for man's gratitude to God and a mention of those occasions, when, sorrowful or rejoicing, or 'sorrowful, yet alway rejoicing' (2 Cor. 6 : 10), the Christian regards thankfulness as still relevant to the circumstances of his life, we shall all the time be setting these themes against the background of a wider, deeper and altogether higher range of spiritual experience. Thanksgiving itself is inseparable from other partial expressions of human response to the love of God.

A *general Thanksgiving* may be followed as a guide along spiritual avenues whose goal is adoration. Vital and essential as thanksgiving is to the existence and growth of the spiritual life, it is not supreme. We can only maintain our insights into its reality and richness if we subsume all beneath the over-riding claims of adoration as paramount in our total response to God. Among the most majestic statements of this conviction during the present century is that by Baron Friedrich von Hügel (1852–1925).

'We men need God much more than, and very differently from, the way and degree in which God needs us. God is the Absolute Cause, the Sole True End and Determiner of our existence, of our persistence, of our nature, of our essential calls and requirements. . . . Thus the positions between God and Man, and between Man and God, are entirely uninter-changeable. Hence the most fundamental need, duty, honour and happiness of man is not petition, nor even contrition, nor again even thanksgiving; these three kinds of prayer which, indeed, must never disappear out of our spiritual lives; but *adoration.*' [8] Again, 'I want you to hold very clearly the *otherness* of God, and the littleness of men. If you don't get that you can't have adoration, and you cannot have religion without adoration.' [9] And, 'The first and central act of religion is *adoration,* sense of God.' [10]

Thanks and praise are among the peak moments in the Christian's experience of God. Their height reaches far above the lower levels of much, if not of most, in the life of man ; yet both of these, as other acts of discipleship or devotion, are dwarfed by adoration which along the mountain range of the spiritual life towers over all. Ultimately, therefore, it is neither thanks nor praise to which we devote ourselves, but 'selfless adoration, awestruck worship as the ruling temper of our life and all we do.' [11]

[8] F. von Hügel, *Essays and Addresses on the Philosophy of Religion,* Second Series, 1930, p. 224.
[9] *Letters from Baron Friedrich von Hügel to a Niece,* ed. G. Greene, 1929, p. xvii.
[10] F. von Hügel, *Selected Letters 1896–1924,* ed. B. Holland, 1928, p. 261.
[11] E. Underhill, *Abba,* 1940, p. 6.

Adoration, springing from praise, marks the opening of
A general Thanksgiving. In the last of his 'Seven Sermons on
Hosea, Chapter XIV,' the author of our prayer declared :

> The true and ultimate end of righteous man, is Almighty
> God, as most glorious in himself, and most good unto us ;
> or the seeking of his glory, that he may be honoured by us ;
> and of our own salvation, that we may be glorified by him.
> The fruition of him as the highest and first *in genere veri,*
> and the greatest and last *in genere boni,* the chiefest object
> for the mind its rest in him by knowledge, and the heart by
> love : this must needs be the best of all ends, both in regard
> of the excellency of it, as being infinitely and most abso-
> lutely good ; and in regard of eternity,—so that the soul,
> having once the possession of it, can never be to seek of
> that happiness which flows from it.[12]

Reynolds is here paraphrasing the accepted teaching of the
mediaeval schoolmen, and he refers in his footnotes to Augustine with special reference to the maxim from the *Confessions,*
'Thou hast made us for thyself : and our heart is unquiet
until it rests in thee.' It is the background of the first words
in the *Thanksgiving.*

'Almighty God, Father.' There is a doctrinal ring in the
words, inevitably leading to adoration, as the terminus of any
Christian statement of doctrine about God. Such prayer, it
has been observed, 'is doctrine translated and made alive in
terms of love and loving knowledge—notice how easily the
first Article of our Religion turns itself into adoration.' [13] The
principle, a guiding rule in prayer, holds of any of the
standard definitions of Christian faith. The Apostles' Creed

[12] *Works,* Vol. III, p. 104.
[13] J. H. Byrom, 'Classics of Mystical and Ascetical Theology' in
Theology, February 1960, p. 56.

or the Nicene Creed similarly 'turns itself into adoration. The process more easily happens when the formula of faith is already in use in an act of affirmation; so, too, in supplication or thanksgiving. It can occur with immediacy and spontaneity in the use of the three opening words of our prayer where 'Almighty God, Father' recalls the 'God, the Father Almighty' of the Apostles' Creed. The similarity in phrase summons the worshipper to the full wonder of the combined moods of approach, affirmation, adoration.

There is here no hint of a desire to limit our insight into the nature and being of God. No special attribute of God is mentioned, no particular act which stimulates the soul to adore. Solely the gaze is set on God in all the fullness and perfection of his nature as our 'true and ultimate end.'

This opening phrase follows the pattern of collects in the Book of Common Prayer where the attention is directed to God before any supplication or thanksgiving is offered; but in the Prayer Book the usual practice is to rehearse only one aspect of revelation which in any particular case calls forth the appropriate response from the worshipper or the worshipping church. This is especially noticeable when the collect commemorates a festival or anniversary.

'Almighty God, who hast given us thy only-begotten Son to take our nature upon him, and as at this time to be born of a pure virgin' (Christmas Day).

'O God, who by the leading of a star didst manifest thy only-begotten Son to the Gentiles' (The Epiphany).

'Almighty God, who through thine only-begotten Son Jesus Christ hast overcome death, and opened unto us the gate of everlasting life' (Easter Day).

A similar method is observed on those occasions when it is desired to stress a particular quality of God.

'Almighty and everlasting God, who hatest nothing that thou hast made and dost forgive the sins of all them that are penitent' (Ash Wednesday).

'Almighty God, who shewest to them that be in error the

light of thy truth, to the intent that they may return into the way of righteousness' (Easter III).

'O God, who hast prepared for them that love thee such good things as pass man's understanding' (Trinity VI).

In the case of a Saint's Day the act of God in the saint's life or the virtue of the saint in question is called to mind.

The role of these opening clauses is the same : to catch the attention of the worshipper, to attach it to God, and to achieve this by concentrating on one theme which is within the worshipper's capacity. Having thus secured the worshipper's attention, the clause stimulates praise. From this moment of praise we move swiftly to the petition which forms the central section of the prayer.

This part of the prayer 'often contains a reference to some Divine attribute, some manifestation of Divine mercy, some revelation of the Divine mind and will, or some fact in the economy of Divine grace; as if to remind us that a God who is really prayed to must be a God who is practically knowable and known.' [14]

'To begin *from* God, and to consider how he meets his creatures, not to begin from some mere chance feeling of ours, and consider how we may work ourselves into a right state' [15] —is the process which is adopted.

The process is unaltered whether the prayer is offered by an individual or by the church collectively. But in those instances where the Collect is prayed individually the process can be made more deliberate and is therefore more easily recognized and shared. Thus, the Christian who uses a Church Collect in his own private worship can linger sufficiently over the opening clause before passing on to the petition, and this pause enables him to make explicit the act of praise which is implied. But the act of praise is there, whether the Collect is prayed individually or collectively, meditatively

[14] W. Bright, 'On the Collects' in *Prayer-Book Commentary,* ed. F. E. Warren, 1933, p. 82.

[15] F. D. Maurice, *The Prayer-Book and the Lord's Prayer,* 1880, p. 157.

C

or swiftly. Indeed, the result of many individuals using a Collect in the more deliberate way in their own private prayers could be that when the Collect is offered in the liturgy of the Church those many individual Christians, now forming a congregation, will be offering together as a common act of worship numerous acts of praise which they have already found in their meditations.

The point for us to notice is that, if the rehearsal of one act or attribute of God is adequate to arouse praise from the worshipper, whether individually or corporately, the use of a general act of recollection in which no specific item in revelation but instead the whole range is included, is capable of stirring that praise many times over. This is the significance of the opening to *A general Thanksgiving*. The *Thanksgiving* is to be *General* in the sense that it is to be the response of the worshipper to all the bounty of God, as distinct from particular thanksgivings in which only one or several of the causes for gratitude are recalled. Therefore its opening clause avoids all suggestion of limiting the scope of what is to be borne in mind. The following clauses will set out the various themes in order. At the start God is addressed without qualification as 'Almighty' and 'Father.' To insert adjectives at this point would be to impose boundaries on what is being contemplated and to set limitations on the praise. On many other occasions in worship we need additional phrases such as those which characterize the Prayer Book Collects. Our need of them arises as much from our own inability to focus our attention upon the divine being if we have not a reminder of his acts or attributes to assist us as from the appropriateness of the reminder to some particular occasion. But when the absence of such additional wording is due, not to the fact that acts and attributes of God are being forgotten, but to the intention to include all of them within the sweep of the worshipper's vision, then the act of praise which is about to begin can outshine all others. To open a prayer of thanksgiving with such brevity is to be exposed to the full brilliance of God's glory, and to kneel in unreserved and unqualified devotion. It is significant that Joseph Addison (1672–1719), whose approach to personal religion was consistently marked by the restraint and balance of reason prevalent in the eighteenth century, hit upon this fact in his fervent hymn.

> When all thy mercies, O my God,
>   My rising soul surveys,
> Transported with the view I'm lost
>   In wonder, love, and praise.

Not even Wesley's use of the last line of this verse, in his own hymn, 'Love divine, all loves excelling,' can exceed the tone of adoration excited by the mention of *all* the mercies of God, an echo of the *General Thanksgiving*'s 'Father of all mercies.'

Praise which is thus expressed cannot be far from adoration. It will at times out-strip its own words, as in the 'high hour of visitation from the living God' which Wordsworth noted.

> No thanks he breathed; he proffered no request;
> Rapt into still communion that transcends
> The imperfect offices of prayer and praise,
> His mind was a thanksgiving to the power
> That made him; it was blessedness and love.[16]

This praise evokes from us the attitude of Thomas Traherne's poem, 'Silence,' in which we set ourselves

>   . . . to view
> His sacred treasures, to admire, rejoice,
> Sing praises with a sweet and heavenly voice,
> See, prize, give hearty thanks within, and love
> Which is the high and only work, above
> Them all.

[16] William Wordsworth (1770–1850), *The Excursion.*

The soul thus engaged undoubtedly adores; for 'the prayer of praise and thanksgiving bears always a contemplative character: he who prays is realizing the greatness, power, holiness and goodness of God.' [17]

5

Adoration is proclaimed at the start of our *Thanksgiving* by addressing God as 'Almighty.' But unfortunately this term has lost its majestic and otherworldly reference as a result of its association in the minds of modern worshippers with discussions about God's omnipotence. It has become a debating point, rather than a call to worship. For us it is an argumentative word, scarcely a term of adoration; and we require to make a deliberate effort if we are to recall the old aura of wonder which the word once possessed.

Professor Burnaby has summarized in masterly fashion this ancient significance of the word.

The word 'almighty' in the Creed translates the Greek *pantocrator* and the Latin *omnipotens*. The Greek word is very rare outside the Bible. It never occurs in prose except in late inscriptions as an epithet of deities such as Hermes or Isis. In the Septuagint, the Greek Translation of the Old Testament, it stands in the great majority of cases for *Sabaoth* in the divine title 'Lord of Hosts.' Jehovah Sabaoth seems originally to have meant the God of the armies of Israel, but later was taken as referring to the 'heavenly hosts,' the armies of angels. In the prophets, the title expresses simply the superhuman might and majesty of Jehovah. *Omnipotens* similarly is a divine epithet in Latin poetry, . . . It is not a word of prose, still less of philosophy. Neither the Greek word nor the Latin convey the strict notion of 'omnipotence' as commonly understood,

[17] F. Heiler, *Prayer*, 1932, p. 318.

36

. . . power to do anything, or even power to do whatever is willed. They are adjectives of 'glorification,' which in the mouth of the suppliant or worshipper express little more than the contrast between human weakness and divine strength.[18]

The author is writing from the doctrinal point of view. Our own approach is that of the worshipper. This difference would perhaps justify us in amending the final sentence of the paragraph which we have quoted; for the upshot of his analysis of what 'Almighty' can mean will be that it is a word which in our mouths will express *nothing less* 'than the contrast between human weakness and divine strength.' This meaning of the title, once rediscovered, amounts to a reinsertion of it into the heavenly context and life of Christian worship.

The use of the title as 'a word of prose' or 'of philosophy' will continue to weaken it unless it is kept within this setting; but in changing it back into an adjective of 'glorification' we cannot jettison what has been gained from its place in thought.

This word has been tested in argument and has not been found wanting as a description of the Creator. To assert omnipotence of God is not to claim that he possesses an erratic ability to do every conceivable thing. The Creator does not, for instance, create a being greater than himself. He does not produce a black whiteness or a square circle. He does not and cannot contradict himself. There are laws, some of which are discernible by man, to which he is subject, yet these laws are not limitations of his greatness for they are the expression of his wisdom, and to these laws of his own devising he has willed that he himself submits. That he acts within the boundaries of these laws is no evidence of weakness. On the contrary, his ability to do so without the errors or misjudgments of which man is conscious is a sign of greatness. It is the absence of irrationality, fickleness, failure on the part of God which in fact illustrates his omnipotence. He,

[18] John Burnaby, *The Belief of Christendom*, 1959, p. 27.

unlike man, can do all that he wills. To that extent he, unlike man, is omnipotent, almighty. This remains an axiom in Christian thought about God, and man can see that not even his own sinful deeds and tendencies which frustrate and can delay, but not destroy, the will of God can invalidate this truth about him.

But 'Almighty' has been used as an adjective in thinking about God only because it was first used in worshipping him. Worship is where this word belongs, and its absence from worship can never be more than a temporary exile. Having been examined and tested in Christian thought, it can be welcomed back into Christian worship. Having been found to be not contrary to reason, it can now be recognized as soaring far beyond all reason. The Christian can unreservedly make use of it to glorify God in his unrestricted adoration of the 'Lord of hosts.'

This adoring salutation of 'Almighty God' is completed by addressing him as 'Father of all mercies.' The dominant thought here is of a permanent property of God. As is said in the Prayer of Humble Access which was added by the English reformers to the Communion Service, God always is 'the same Lord, whose property' (meaning 'nature') 'is always to have mercy.' In scripture he is spoken of not only as 'Father of mercies' (2 Cor. 1 : 3), but also as 'the Father of lights' (Jas. 1 : 17) and 'the Father of glory' (Ephes. 1 : 17). An unchanging quality, which can be recognized on all occasions and in all circumstances is being asserted. Always merciful, he is 'Father of all mercies.' But this phrase is more than descriptive. Because we are speaking of God we imply, when we assert of him some quality which does not change, that he is the originator of it. He is the fount of 'lights,' of 'glory,' of 'all mercies.' When we speak of him as Father of his 'only-begotten Son' Jesus Christ we are referring to a particular, although divine, parenthood, which is contained within the mystery of the threefold Godhead, the Holy and Undivided Trinity. But when we now speak of him as 'Father' of 'mercies' we are affirming the heavenly parent's supply to his children of blessings which indeed he pours from his inner being. He is himself the source and origin of those qualities which he displays. A twofold fatherhood in God is here indicated : he is the Father of all men, as Creator, and he is Father of all mercies, as Perfect Being whose perfections derive from himself.

6

Mercies are the active expressions of mercy, which is an attitude of patience, forbearance and compassion towards the weak on the part of any one who is powerful. These gifts, benefits, blessings the recipient for his part has no power whatever to earn, win or deserve. The mercy may be material or spiritual, visible or invisible, large or small, wanted or unwanted, expected or unexpected. It is always totally unmerited. Mercies are neither wages, nor rewards, nor prizes. Their being given depends entirely upon the donor, their being received depends only secondarily, and by way of response, upon the receiver.

To be at the mercy of someone is to be in that person's power. The head of a state—whether crowned sovereign or elected president—can have mercy on criminals. A commander in the field can have mercy on his prisoners-of-war. Victorious nations have it in their power to show mercy towards the defeated enemy. In human relationships mercy is regularly made possible by the possession of authority or influence. But in normal human relationships, the power is limited and the mercies correspondingly restricted : it is only where excessive power is claimed, as by a despot or dictator, that the humanity in mercy is violated and there is no willingness to grant mercy at all.

Human examples of mercy, however dramatic or timely, are partial illustrations of the divine. They correspond to limited power and therefore display only some mercies. From God alone, who is 'Almighty,' can come 'all mercies.' There is no limit to the variety or the range of the mercies of God; for his majesty has no bounds, and 'as his majesty is, so is his mercy' (Ecclus. 2 : 18).

Bishop Reynolds seized upon this truth and repeatedly referred to it as one of the most effective incitements to the Christian's personal life of prayer and discipleship. 'We should keep a catalogue of God's mercies to quicken us unto duty, as well as a catalogue of our own sins, to make us cry for mercy.' [19] 'We can never pray, till we cry "Abba, Father"; we can never call unto him but in the "multitude of his mercies." Even when distressed sinners pray prayer proceeds from apprehension of mercies : for prayer is the child of faith, and the object of faith is mercy.' [20] And our prayers are to be enlarged to correspond with what we know of God's 'abundant mercies.' We are 'to beg for an answer, not according to the defect and narrowness of our own low conceptions, but according to the fulness of God's own abundant mercies. It would not please one of us, if a beggar should ask of us gold, or jewels, silk, or dainties; we should esteem such a petitioner fuller of pride and impudence than of want. But God delights to have his people beg great things of him, to implore the performance of "exceeding great and precious promises" (2 Peter 1 : 4); to pray for a share in the "unsearchable riches of Christ"; to know things which pass knowledge, and to be filled "with the fulness of God" (Ephes. 3 : 8, 16, 19); to ask things which "eye hath not seen, nor ear heard, nor have entered into the heart of man to conceive" (1 Cor. 2 : 9); to ask not as beggars for alms, but as "children for an inheritance" (Rom. 8 : 15, 17, 23; Gal. 4 : 6, 7); not to ask some thing, or a few things, but "in every thing to let our requests be made known unto God" (Phil. 4 : 6); because, with Christ, he giveth us "freely all things" (Rom. 8 : 32);

[19] *Works,* Vol. III, p. 258.
[20] Ibid., p. 306.

even "all things richly to enjoy" (1 Tim. 6 : 17).' Reynolds rounds off this statement by declaring that we are 'to regulate our prayers more by the merits and riches of Christ, and by the greatness of God's mercies, than by those apprehensions which we cannot but have of our own unworthiness.' [21]

Echoes of these passages are to be heard in the author's phrase 'Father of all mercies.' By beginning *A general Thanksgiving* with that phrase he is asserting abundance of mercy in the nature of God.

This divine attribute is absolute, unchanging in intensity, universal in its range. It is firmly demonstrated in scripture. From the Old Testament we have the memorable declaration of it by Isaiah. 'Let the wicked forsake his way, and the unrighteous man his thoughts : and let him return unto the Lord, and he will have mercy upon him; and to our God, for he will abundantly pardon' (Isa. 55 : 7). On this, Matthew Henry notes that the verse means 'He will multiply to pardon . . . as we have multiplied to sin.' Again from the New Testament there is Luke 6 : 36, on which Henry comments :

It is the glory of God that he is kind to the unthankful and evil, bestows the gifts of common providence even upon the worst of men, who are every day provoking him, and rebelling against him, and using those very gifts to his dishonour. . . . This should strongly engage us to be merciful to our brethren, even such as have been injurious to us, not only that God is so to others, but that he is so to us, though we have been, and are, evil and unthankful; it is of his mercies that *we* are not consumed.

Here is the ultimate reason for the command, 'Be ye therefore merciful, as your Father also is merciful,' each attempt to lead the Christian life bringing us back to the 'Father of

[21] *Works*, Vol. III, pp. 326–7.

all mercies.' Thus the *General Thanksgiving,* as F. D. Maurice pointed out, is 'grounded upon an acknowledgement of God's fatherly love to all men' and has as its aim 'that this love may be a bond of union between him and all men.' [22] That 'bond of union' which is ours is renewed and kept firm by thanks and praise when these are lit by the radiance of adoring wonder.

[22] F. D. Maurice, *The Prayer-Book and the Lord's Prayer,* 1880. p. 160.

CHAPTER 3

CREATION

1

Creation is the work solely of God. As such it is unique. In vain we search for adequate parallels to it in human experience, for no human activity can fully share its status. The most that we can do in making a comparison of man with God is to discover in this connection those points where there is at any rate some similarity alongside the immeasureable distance. The vocations of the parent, or of the thinker, artist, inventor; every achievement of the designer, from space rocket to Parisian fashions; cultivation of the soil and the production of new horticultural specimens—in all these spheres and in others there is some resemblance of man to his Maker. In such activities man is conscious that to some extent he is creative. From a given start or in a given situation a new product is brought forth. The new child, new thought, new work of art, new daffodil, is not just a copy of what has been there before. There is a genuine newness in the birth or the making. The potentialities which spring from this element of novelty, hidden in each moment of his life and in each stage of his environment, summon man to exercise and to stretch his creative powers. In his response to the summons he mirrors the divine action and he knows it. But there the similarity ends. For God's work in creation is not response. It includes also the moment or the situation which calls forth the activity from men. Parent, artist, worker are feeble reflections of 'Almighty God' in the immensity of his divine powers. Ultimately the distance between the two is demonstrated by the claim that God himself is uncreated.

Creation is described by Thomas Aquinas as a special kind

of relationship. Here again are seen its uniqueness and its disparity from human action.

Relationships between human beings vary. Some are merely temporary, depending on accidents of time or space : as when a guest sits on his hostess's right at dinner or when a boy is in Mr. Smith's class at school. Others, though temporary, are more closely woven into the stuff of human living, such as the relationships between employer and employee, or between the government and the electorate. More lasting are those between the members of a family, according to which brothers remain brothers long after they have ceased to meet, and grandparents, parents and children remain related even when the older generation has been removed from sight at death. The relationships may indicate equality or differences of rank. The extremes of devotion or of fear may maintain them.

This kaleidoscope of human relationships, which is perpetually changing and producing new patterns of society and behaviour, reveals the permanent stability of our relationship to God. In all our own creative activities we part with that which we produce. The writer finds that his book is no longer a living part of him when it is completed. The sculptor or painter is always pressing on to his next work. The parent, while still related to his child, has to be willing to see the adult son or daughter develop a personality and life which are independent of him. The family must take wing.

But in spite of all that men may imagine to be taking place on the surface of their lives, they cannot acquire a status or power of independent existence apart from their Creator similar to these instances of their independence of one another. They forget or ignore God, but they do not live without him. Their unique relationship to him is one-sided. Their dependence upon him is continuous, and every split second of their existence betrays it. But this dependence is not reversible. Even the parent to some extent needs his children, for the fulfilment of his own personality or for the maintenance of himself in old age, and the artist needs the masterpieces which have left his hand for the fuller flowering of his genius and the more thorough expression of his visions and fertility later. God in no such sense needs his creatures. But all the time all his creatures in every detail need him. There is no thought without the thinking of a thinker : there is no creature without the life of the Creator. 'As long as anything exists, God must be present to it.'[1]

The author of our prayer has given us his own exposition of this doctrine of creation. In his *Annotations on the Book of Ecclesiastes* he comments on 'Remember now thy Creator in the days of thy youth' (chapter 12, verse 1). The word Creator, he observes, includes 'many reasons, why God ought to be remembered and served by us.' Of these reasons he summarizes four.

1. He made us, and not we ourselves; and we owe our service to him from whom we receive our being (Ps. 100 : 2, 3). Remember he made all things for himself : we are *of* him; therefore we must live *to* him (Rev. 1 : 6; Isa. 43 : 21; Rom. 12 : 1, 2 and 14 : 7, 8).

2. He made us after his own image ; to know him, and to have special interest in him, and acquaintance with him : and being made like him, we are obliged unto his services (Ephes. 4 : 23, 24).

3. By that power which created us, we are continually preserved : if he withdraw it, we presently perish : 'In him we live, and move, and have our being.' The more vigour and strength we have, the more sensible we should be of that divine supportance, which continueth it unto us (Acts 17 : 27–30; Ps. 104 : 28, 29).

4. He who hath power to create, hath power to destroy : and he will shew the same almighty power in destroying those, who live not suitably to the ends of their creation (1 Sam. 2 : 6, 8; 2 Thess. 1 : 9). This creating power of God should teach us to fear him (Jer. 5 : 22).[2]

[1] Thomas Aquinas, *Summa Theologica,* I, Q. VIII, art. 1.
[2] *Works,* Vol. IV, pp. 238–9.

Bishop Reynolds here makes no claims to have provided an exhaustive and complete analysis, but he has said enough to indicate that the Christian conception of creation has reference to a great deal more besides the bare beginnings of creatures.

Whenever a Christian talks about creation he is concerned with a mystery which leaps beyond the first remote start of the universe. What causes him the greatest astonishment and wonder is not the fact that the universe has started but that it continues. The existence of the universe now is what really stimulates him to make any enquiry or valuation of it at all and the failure of it to account for its own existence prompts him to the affirmation that the ground for its existence now no less than the ground for its beginning at a stage in time when he could not possibly have been present, is to be identified with God. The universe is named by him the Creation because it not only has come into being but also now continues to be in being as the result of the activity of God. The divine creative work persists each day, and to be created is to be in a state of unique relationship with the Creator, upon whom is placed complete and utter dependence.

In the monastic act of worship at Nones, in full daylight at about two or three o'clock, occur words which have become known to English worshippers in the nineteenth-century translation by the Revd. J. Ellerton and Dr. Hort :

> O Strength and Stay upholding all creation,
> Who ever dost thyself unmoved abide,
> Yet day by day the light in due gradation
> From hour to hour through all its changes guide.

The tense strength of the Latin has here given place to a relaxed Victorian mood, and the English version has become an evening hymn, but the underlying theme has been kept. The Creator is 'the Strength and Stay,' not only the Originator, of all that is. Creation remains as the unique relation-

Creation

ship, depending at every minute upon the act and will of God, who enables his creatures to be.

In our *General Thanksgiving* we are giving thanks that this universal fact of nature applies to ourselves. 'We bless thee for our creation': not merely for the fact that we have been created, that we have been born, or that we began our lives, though that in itself can be taken by some to justify gratitude to God; but also for the fact that we are being continuously created, that we are held in existence, that we are growing, maturing, and ageing, that we are living our lives now. It must be admitted that thus interpreted the thought of persistence is what dominates the mind in attending to creation. It explains the relevance of the *Thanksgiving* to all circumstances and justifies its repetition as an expression of sincere thankfulness on the most varied occasions. Because in creation the marvel for the child or man of faith is not that he himself came into existence ten or fifty or more years ago, but that he is continuing to exist, the expression of his thanks is never redundant. To have said *A general Thanksgiving* a year ago is not the same thing as saying it again to-day. Always and everywhere creation means for him the fact that he exists now. Every new 'now' entitles him to say a new *Thanksgiving*.

The Christian attitude pulsates with this conception of the uninterrupted, ceaselessly flowing, continuous, yet deliberate creative activity of God. Not even the appearance of the set order in nature contradicts this. 'It is not,' William Temple (1881–1944) said, 'that there is a fixed natural order laid down once for all by God, and since left alone, with which from time to time he interferes; it is that all the while he is acting, only all the while it is appropriate, on most occasions, to follow a regular course, as does the ordinary man of regular habit in the conduct of his daily life.' [3] But this aspect of nature is not easily noticed until it is pointed out. The regularity of the seasons, of winter and summer, seed-time and

[3] W. Temple, *The Preacher's Theme To-day*, 1936, p. 16.

47

harvest, has the mask of a routine : in reality it is the rhythm of endless initiative and innovation on the Creator's part within the range of his own purposes or providence.

God's continued creativity is best seen and shared by the Christian in his life of redemption. 'If any man is in Christ, he is a new creature' or, according to the New English Bible, 'When anyone is united to Christ, there is a new world' (2 Cor. 5 : 17). 'Behold, I make all things new' (Rev. 21 : 5). But this newly creative action of God, at work in and on our lives and characters, is itself the original creative power being brought to play upon us in our particular situation as sinful creatures. It presupposes the continuous creation which is from, but not confined to, the beginning of things. The possibility that God in Christ will re-create a man is derived from the fact that all the while he is creating that man. The new heavens, the new earth, the new creature is the completing of a process which is continuous in our natures.

We have a parable of this in the annual renewal of the country-side in spring. This, for all its regularity and apparent repetition, is alive with newness every time. As an anonymous writer for the Bible Reading Fellowship recorded : 'God is continually making new things, giving new life which demands new forms of expression. He does not "do up" last year's primroses : he will make new ones this spring.' The thought can be extended to embrace any human pursuit which on the surface seems to be an example of repetition. The preacher delivering an old sermon, the politician making the same speech, the Christians and the Church using the well-worn prayers are repeating words : but although the words are the same as those which they used before the occasion is different, and because there is a continued life of experience, meaning and conviction at the back of them old words on a new occasion become new. Since they were last spoken, life has moved forward and has been capable of investing them with new meaning and new conviction. Ideally this happens in education, beginning from the time when the

child may learn words by heart as only words and leading on
to the stage when he later learns the truth which the words
convey. They are then in fact

> the words
> That one by one the touch of life
> Has turned to truth.[4]

It happens again in the experience of the concert-goer who
listens to a pianist playing the same concerto which he played
many years previously, but now playing it with an entirely
new fervour and intensity of interpretation. But these are not
exceptional experiences, even though it is exceptional for
modern man to take note of them. Throughout the whole
range of human thought, emotion and action freshness and
novelty are each day breaking through. They are not lost on
those who acknowledge the continuously creative work of God
and 'bless' him 'for our creation.'

2

Awareness of our own createdness leads us on to marvel at
the createdness of the universe. The ease with which we make
this transition in our thought is assisted by our habit of using
the word 'creation' to indicate both the creative activity of
God, and the world of nature as a whole. But our insight into
what this comprehensive createdness means cannot depend on
our accounts of nature. These descriptions have been enlarged
and elaborated in our own day on a scale which exceeds any
possible forecasts which our ancestors could have made. By
climbing seven miles up Everest, by diving seven miles into
the Pacific, by exploring outer space and hitting the moon,
by control of the air and of distant communication, by tele-
scope and microscope, and by whatever new discovery is
made to-morrow or the day after to-morrow, we have at our

[4] H. J. Newbolt (1862–1938), *Clifton Chapel.*

D

disposal more information about the created order than any previous generation. But insight is not automatically assisted by information; analysis is not necessarily the prelude to appreciation. Man can continue to amass his statistics without attending to the significance of what he is measuring, and this process can conceivably continue until our own century will appear to be as ill-informed to men of a later age as, say, the first century now appears to ourselves. We remain predominantly ignorant men if we have no insight into what createdness means.

The believer in God attempts to maintain a view which, while independent of the increase of information about the created world, welcomes every development which is the fruit of honest enquiry and experiment, and at the same time gives to every new road of discovery its own significance. The more he is told about the component parts of the universe, the more readily he is able to respond with a view which throws over that universe a perpetual sense of wonder. To the dry results of analysis he is able to add the blaze of appreciation.

While therefore we hold ourselves ready at any time to welcome with eagerness the wealth of detail which modern enquiry can supply about the universe, we need not wait until the complete stock of information has been catalogued before we reach our estimate of what the universe is. Detail fill in the gaps in a general view, but we already have our view. It is possible to admire a mountain without any of the scientific information which can now be acquired about it. The information when available adds depth and intensity to a wonder which is already ours. The same observation will apply to our attitude to the smallest living creature or the most minute particle. Admiration is independent of scale. And within the mind of the believer every experience of admiration for nature is the prelude to thanksgiving for it.

The Christian discovers that thanks or praise to God for creation is communicated from one person to another like enthusiasm.

Creation

A graphic illustration appears in a sermon, published at the turn of the century, by Bishop Phillips Brooks (1835–93). He is expounding 'the interpreting power of great enthusiastic men' who 'bring out the value of things so that other men can see them.'

> This is what happens when you walk through a great picture gallery with a true artist. At first you are surprised, perhaps you are disgusted at yourself. You feel yourself praising the pictures that he praises and having no eyes for anything which he passes by with indifference. You say, 'I have no mind of my own. I am his mere echo. I do not really like these things, I am only trying to like them because he does.' But very possibly you are wrong. It is very likely that your artist companion is revealing to you what you are perfectly capable of appreciating, although you are not capable of discovering it.

Appreciation of nature within the context of faith is parallel to this. The predicament of modern man is that he finds himself placed in an environment which far exceeds his own powers of measurement or valuation. In this 'great picture gallery' he has to decide upon whom he will ask to show him round. In his present stage of appreciation he has, it seems, already invited the technician, the biologist, the physicist, the chemist. Another available guide is the believer who maintains that the 'great picture gallery' of nature belongs to God and is a compelling demonstration of his creative power. It is this guide who completes what the others have to say and can lead us to the fully satisfying appreciation which is known to be real and lasting.

> That it is real appreciation and not mere imitation you will feel sure when by and by you go back alone to the picture and find that still, though he is no longer with you, the charm which you felt in it through him remains. He has not blinded but enlightened your perceptions.[5]

[5] Phillips Brooks, *The Light of the World and Other Sermons*, 1899, p. 328.

This experiment is so intimately woven into human experience that other similar accounts come from quite different environments. Thus, a modern philosopher, George Santayana, described how he accompanied a friend who was expert in art appreciation through some of the world's great galleries. His friend would stand, entranced, in front of a masterpiece; and he would himself share in the experience of gazing at it. Then,

> My own load was lifted, and I saw how instrumental were all the labour and history of man, to be crowned, if crowned at all, only in intuition.[6]

It is for the Christian to follow the lead of this illustration and to search for someone who, like 'a true artist,' can be his escort through the universe interpreted as God's 'great picture gallery.' He requires a friend through whose experience his own 'load' is 'lifted.' He needs someone who can teach him in the first place how to look and in the second place where to look.

This, in point of fact, is the function of the Christian's guide because it is a supreme role of the Christian Church. 'Religion,' it cannot be too often insisted, 'is bound up with the contemplative attitude. . . . If the Church can get people to *look at* anything, rather than use it or talk about it, we have at least achieved *le premier pas*. Let them look at even the beauties of sense, or, by a more intricate process, wonder at the human soul : then they may be able to make religious ideas their own . . . they may come to be able to *look at* even the images of God.'[7] Looking leads to praising or giving thanks; thus any guide who on the Church's behalf shows us how to look is ultimately showing us how to praise.

For this reason we need not suppose that we can amass all available information about creation only from what scien-

6 George Santayana, *The Middle Span*, 1945, p. 142.
7 Geddes MacGregor, *Aesthetic Experience in Religion*, 1947, p. 227.

tists said about it yesterday. We have also to take into account what believers have been saying—or rather singing—about it for centuries. This is the way in which our thanksgivings for it are to be learnt. By following the stanzas of a Christian's praise we are allowing ourselves to be conducted on a tour through this vast 'picture gallery' of God and we are putting ourselves in the position of sharing, and eventually of making our own, the enthusiasm which is expressed in the religious language of delight.

Pæans of praise and songs of thankfulness for creation have been accumulating from the earliest stages of our religion. The Bible and Prayer Book contain timeless specimens, which have their echoes in our own literature. Well-known examples are : Psalm 103, repeated in 'Praise, my soul, the king of heaven' by H. F. Lyte (1793–1847); Psalm 104, and the version 'O worship the Lord' by R. Grant (1779–1838); Psalm 136 and the poem 'Let us, with a gladsome mind' by John Milton (1608–74); Psalm 148, with the versions 'Praise the Lord of heaven' by T. B. Browne (1805–74) and 'Praise the Lord! ye heavens, adore him' in the Foundling Hospital Collection (1796); Psalm 150; and the *Benedicite omnia opera,* to be found in its fullest form in the Song of the Three Children in the Apocrypha.

These, and others, may be regarded as pattern acts of private praise, as well as expressions of corporate worship. They have been overlooked by Christians not only because they are numerous, but also, and perhaps chiefly, because their use in the worship of church has tended to obscure their personal nature. In private praise our method will be to take one of these at a time, to dwell on it, to offer it slowly from the heart, and to repeat it often. Later it can be discarded, and the worshipper can return to meditate upon creation itself. He now has an 'appreciation' of the mystery of creation which is his own, although the 'discovery' of it has been made by the psalmist or poet before him. By using another's psalm or hymn of praise for creation he has reached his own personal awareness of what createdness is.

After 'creation,' 'preservation.' The association of these two words in our *Thanksgiving* has become so familiar that it has ceased to cause any surprise. Yet a question arises as soon as the connection between the two is examined : for if Reynolds considered that creation includes preservation we are bound to ask why he mentioned them both. Is this simply an instance of the use of double terms when one would have done, a sacrifice of exactness for the sake of rhythm, or even a surrender to verbosity?

Analysis of what is meant by both words suggests that our author was being deliberate in using them both, and that each represents a distinct reason for our 'humble and hearty thanks' to 'Almighty God.'

A parallel to the use of the two words in *A general Thanksgiving* is provided by the *Prayer for All Sorts and Conditions of Men,* where God is addressed as 'the Creator and Preserver of all mankind.' This prayer is attributed to Peter Gunning (1614–84), later Bishop of Ely, who attended the Savoy Conference as an anglican contemporary of Reynolds. It was contributed to the Book of Common Prayer at the revision of 1661, at the same time as the *Thanksgiving.* The identity in date and place invites us to assume that they were not entirely unrelated. Bishop Gunning's phrase is attributing to God two roles : that of Creator, and that of Mankind's Preserver. God is called Creator by virtue of the power by which he has brought into existence and maintains in existence the whole universe : he is named Preserver because amongst creatures man is a special object of his protection. Bishop Reynolds in the Thanksgiving is employing the two words, 'creation' and 'preservation,' in a manner which is compatible with this interpretation : for while in a special sense man may know that he is embraced by the love of God, 'preserved,' he knows also that he is among those creatures whose existence in general is dependent on God, 'created.' It is neither unreasonable nor verbose on our part to 'bless' God for both 'creation' and 'preservation.'

But what is it which according to the Christian view differentiates this 'preservation' from 'creation'? In what sense can the Christian claim that he is not only created, but also preserved, by God?

The Prayer Book enlightens us on this point. The general view of our Liturgy, taken as a whole, is that creation refers to this life, preservation to the next : the Creator is God as the One on whom as living creatures we depend for life, the Preserver is the same God as the One on whom we depend for eternal life. When we say that God creates man, both in body and soul, we have in mind primarily although not exclusively the body ; when we say that God preserves man, similarly in body and soul, we have in mind, again primarily and not exclusively, the soul. In numerous contexts the Prayer Book mentions 'preserve' or 'preservation' with an emphasis upon the soul or eternal life or both, and when the body is mentioned in this context the thought is of the 'spiritual body' (1 Cor. 15 : 44), and consequently of the resurrection of the body.

In the Communion the Sacrament is given with the words 'preserve thy body and soul unto everlasting life.'

At Confirmation the concluding collect is that, as the result of God's protection 'both now and ever, we may be preserved in body and soul.'

At Marriage the first blessing of the bride and bridegroom includes 'preserve and keep you . . . that in the world to come ye may have life everlasting.'

In the Psalter we have : 'preserve him from this generation for ever' (12 : 7); 'alway preserve me' (40 : 14); 'dwell before God for ever . . . preserve him' (61 : 7); 'preserve my life from fear of the enemy' (64 : 1); 'preserve the souls of the poor' (72 : 13); 'preserve thou those that are appointed to die' (79 : 11); 'preserve thou my soul, for I am holy' (86 : 2); 'the Lord shall preserve thee from all evil : yea, it is he that shall keep thy soul' (121 : 7). As used in Christian worship, these verses undeniably contain a primarily spiritual meaning. Although originally some of the texts may have referred only to physical preservation from dangers or enemies, their Christian interpretation extends further. The 'enemies' are spiritual, the 'preservation' is spiritual. In the mood of a Christian's worship it is the spiritual preservation which is the dominant theme when such verses are repeated. Further, because in certain instances this spiritual interpretation of 'preservation' is beyond question, the worshipper extends the thought to those instances where the mood in itself is not explicity connected with either 'soul' or 'life everlasting.' Constantly there is this association of words in the Christian's mind. In general use 'preservation' has come to mean preservation to eternity. Consequently, while we may use the word 'creation' to signify God's continuous love for all creation, we may use the word 'preservation' to signify this special and specific favour for man.[8]

In blessing God for our creation and preservation, therefore, we are thanking him for a double demonstration of his 'loving-kindness towards us.' Having been created and while held in being in this world, we are preserved for life in the next. As created we are recipients of a divine love which we share with all creatures in the universe ; as preserved we are recipients of a divine love which we share with our fellow-men, but only with them. And our 'preservation,' no less than our 'creation,' can be counted amongst the 'blessings of this life,' for although its fulfilment and complete enjoyment must be reserved for the hereafter its bestowal belongs to the here and now. It is within this life that we are made aware of our

[8] The description of God in the First of the Thirty Nine Articles as 'the preserver of all things' does not invalidate this general interpretation of the meaning of the English Prayer Book; for, (i) the Articles are not part of the Book of Common Prayer, but an appendix to it ; (ii) they are a century earlier than our completed Book, and (iii) their infrequent use need not have affected the interpretation which has arisen from the regular use of the Prayer Book itself.

status as not only created, but also saved, redeemed, pre-served. 'The Continuation of the World, though fallen,' wrote William Law (1686–1761), 'is a glorious Proof and Instance of the Goodness of God, that so a Race of new-born Angels may be brought forth in it. Happy therefore is it, that we have such a World as this to be born into, since we are only born, to be born again to the Life of Heaven.' [9]

[9] W. Law, *The Spirit of Prayer*, 1749, p. 90.

CHAPTER 4

PAIN

1

The one phrase in *A general Thanksgiving* which can irritate twentieth century man is 'all the blessings of this life.' Reference to 'Almighty God,' whose nature and acts are known in creation and history, he may scarcely notice. Mention of the 'goodness' and the 'loving-kindness' of God he will be prepared to let pass. But an over-all allusion to blessings as though these were the normal and natural features of his life he will not be disposed to leave unchallenged. He will reflect that, even if material prosperity in some quarters has notably increased and the general standard of living, at least in the West, has been dramatically lifted since the devastation of war-time, he cannot himself turn a blind eye to the vast stretches of misery which remain. Poverty, hunger, nuclear terror haunt a large proportion of the human race. The paradox of the modern situation is that those individuals who are most enslaved to the material standards of the day, are able at the same time to be among the first to protest that others do not share their advantages, and also among the least willing to do the sharing. The 'haves' find that they can be angry at the plight of the 'have-nots' without being conspicuous in helping to relieve them. But there is a further outcry at the existence of hardship in modern life. Improvements in world health have progressed alongside an increasing sensitiveness to suffering. Even where the sufferers are kept out of sight behind the impersonal walls of welfare institutions they are not banished from the mind. Modern man tries to forget the crippled and handicapped in vain. By the very fact that the extent of pain may have been diminished, its intensity is the more acutely felt. Men still suffer. The unbeliever who is invited to give thanks for 'all the blessings of this life' is the first to seize upon this fact. His anger against life is based on his knowledge that by no means all the things of this life are in his view blessings.

In our *Thanksgiving* there is no mention of suffering; but suffering is not omitted. The faithful Christian in the very act of praising God knows that sufferers are always with him, and the Christian whose vocation is to suffer knows that during his own sufferings he can continue to give thanks. Praise and pain are inseparable in the rhythm of the Christian life.

In giving thanks for creation we are confronted with a world which presents us with much else besides sunsets, quiet landscapes and spring flowers. The American Episcopal Church uses the passage about the lilies of the field as the Gospel at the Communion on Thanksgiving Day, as though naïvely to suggest that everything in God's garden is lovely; but this is to be qualified by another interpretation which also comes from the United States.

The 'sad American, Paul Elmer More, who tried to combine Platonism with Christianity' [1] was drawing attention to it when he described his visit to Symond's Yat, the beauty-spot in Wales.

To the eye it was a widespread theatre of joy, and a masque of peaceful beauty. Until I thought of what lay beneath the surface. Here, in fact, was an army of countless individuals, each driven on by an instinctive lust of life as if engaged on a vast internecine warfare—each blade of grass fighting for its place under the sun and obtaining it by the suppression of some other plant, each animal preying for sustenance upon some other form of life. It is a system of ruthless competition and remorseless extermination. . . . From every spot of the earth rises continually the battle-cry of Nature : *Vae victis.* [2]

[1] H. L. Short in *The Hibbert Journal,* October 1960, p. 84.
[2] P. E. More, *The Sceptical Approach to Religion,* 1934, pp. 78–80. Quoted by H. H. Farmer, *The World and God,* 1935, pp. 279–80, and by H. Davies, *Christian Deviations,* 1954, pp. 117–18 (but omitted from 1961 edition).

The Christian will keep company with the humanist in peering like this 'beneath the surface,' for he knows that on innumerable occasions he is confronted with nature 'red in tooth and claw' without any kind of disguise. A Christian missionary in India testified :

> No one has ever seen a cobra viciously turn, spread out its hood, hiss and strike, without being conscious of something devilish present, a devil's thought not God's thought.[3]

But if our gaze penetrates as far as this in nature, so must our praise. We must discover an approach which will embrace the most daunting and frightening episodes of suffering or evil within the range of our thanksgiving, if we mean our thanksgiving to be offered to 'the one, true God.' Otherwise while we are holding ourselves ready to recognize and welcome the divine presence in 'the still, small voice' or 'the sound of stillness' we shall be banishing the Creator from the wind and fire and earthquake. The Christian's struggle is to place his belief in God as 'maker of all things visible and invisible' and at the same time to love and trust him without any sort of reserve or qualification as the God of love.

This inner struggle, experienced by the man who would reconcile the power and the love of God, is swept away by the sense of compulsion which the Christian receives when he transfers his attention to Christ.

The God of the Bible is not One who is remote. He is the God of history, actively involved in its events, intimately concerned with its men and women. Before Christ we have the record of his acts amongst mankind, from then onwards of his acts with humanity. His interior working inside human nature, starting from the incarnation of the Son, entails a share in the whole range of experience of his sons and daughters. The wounds of the Crucified show that suffering is not shut out from this. The life of Christ may not enable

[3] W. H. T. Holmes, *The Presence of God,* 1923, p. 8.

us with absolute certainty to see suffering in God, but it does open the road for us to meet God in suffering. Christ has borne not only our griefs and our sorrows and our sins, but also our illnesses and pains. This is one clear result of his Cross. Our fears that suffering separates us from our Maker prove to be groundless, and we need not wait for any further justification for giving God thanks in pain.

2

No Christian can let go the conviction that pain can be used for a purpose. In the hands of God those elements in his world which appear to rebel against his rule can be bent to his will. The greatness of God is such that, as Augustine taught, he can turn to good that which opposes him, bringing good out of evil. The comprehensive claim that all things work together for good to them that love God has more justification than a superficial critic is willing to admit. The Lord loves those whom he chastens. He disciplines men, as a parent does children. As gold in the furnace, so man is tested, because so man is valued; and God will go on polishing his most precious metal until he can see his face, his own image, in it.[4] 'God is sufficiently wise and good and powerful and merciful to turn even the most apparently disastrous events to the advantage and profit of those who humbly adore and accept his will in all that he permits.'[5]

An acted parable of this truth in our religion is contained in the story of Joseph. Addressing his brothers after the failure of their plot against him which led to his own astonishing preservation and promotion to honour and success, he told them, 'Ye thought evil against me; but God meant it unto good, to bring to pass, as it is this day, to save much people.'[6] Matthew Henry's comment on the verse presents this as an

---

[4] See Amy Carmichael, *Rose from Briar*, 1933, p. 29.
[5] J. P. de Caussade, *Abandonment*, Letter X, 1921 ed., p. 118.
[6] Gen. 50: 20.

instance of the overruling of evil and as an occasion for praise.

> When God makes use of men's agency for the performance of his counsels, it is common for him to mean one thing and them another, even the quite contrary; but God's counsel shall stand. See Isa. 10 : 7. Again, often God brings good out of evil, and promotes the designs of his providence even by the sins of men; not that he is the author of sin, far be it from us to think so; but, his infinite wisdom overrules events, and directs the chain of them, that in the issue, that ends in his praise which in its own nature had a direct tendency to his dishonour.

The reference in the text from Isaiah is not without its own special relevance to a century such as our own in which the dictator has become an embodiment of evil. Isaiah is speaking of Sennacherib, King of Assyria, as raised up to be God's instrument, 'howbeit he meaneth not so, neither doth his heart think so.' On this Matthew Henry repeats his affirmation of the prevailing providence of God. 'The wise God often makes even the sinful passions and projects of men subservient to his own great and holy purposes,' and 'when God makes use of men as instruments in his hand to do his work it is very common for *him* to mean one thing and *them* to mean another, nay, for them to mean quite the contrary to what he intends.' But, quotes Henry again, 'the counsel of the Lord that shall stand.'[7]

Scripture firmly holds to this doctrine of the ultimate defeat of evil. What in the hands of human enemies are evil threatening and for a time frustrating our safety or serenity become in the hands of our Maker methods by which he moulds us, and those pains and sufferings which bear no trace of human origin can be no less his own means for making and multiplying good.

[7] Prov. 19 : 21.

In the mind of a Christian blessings of a special kind are to be included in 'all the blessings of this life.' These are spiritual blessings, like the forgiveness of sins, a quiet mind, the trusting heart and lasting friendship between Christians. They do not depend on material prosperity, national prestige, or a happy family life. To a certain extent the recipients' circumstances are irrelevant to them, although they are not irrelevant to the circumstances. They are to be accepted in the circumstances of particular situations, but they are not produced by these.

The universal missionary impetus of the Christian Church is a perpetual witness to this priority of spiritual blessings. The gospel of God is being spread amongst all men regardless of their wealth or work, nationality or name. All equally are capable of accepting it. Nevertheless, although the worship, including the praise and thanksgiving, of an individual or community is not dependent on circumstances, that offering is made from the centre of these circumstances. Environment is there as part of the rough, unshaped, raw material which is to be turned into the dedicated offering of penitence or praise. One positive value of suffering is that it can be turned into a means by which Christian character is formed. So, too, material conditions, whether soft or hard, can become occasions or opportunities for the bestowal and acceptance of the spiritual blessings which compose Christian salvation. The Christian claims that this is particularly the case when the conditions are of hardship and misfortune. It is then that the clash in colour is most vivid, and the spiritual blessing together with the praise which it inspires will shine with greatest brilliance.

3

It is difficult to say which is the greater wonder : the transformation of the sufferer who in the process of praise becomes the radiant saint, or the transformation of the suffering until by praise it becomes the accompaniment to blessings. Whenever we encounter a dedicated Christian sufferer we witness both these wonders at work. On the one hand, there is the joy of the sufferer, sometimes vivacious, sometimes actually gay, sometimes calm, certainly at peace with self and God, possessing a joy which is utterly real. On the other hand, there are the positive graces, benefits, blessings, received in the state of suffering, embracing both sufferer and suffering in the firm and lasting love of God.

Examples of the reality of this experience of pain have multiplied during the centuries of Christian faith, but even these, for all their number, give only a limited view of its full extent. We are here concerned with an experience of believers of whom many have no capacity for expressing in words the profundity of that which they are sharing; and others if they once possessed such capacity have lost it as the result of their state of suffering. Yet in spite of this limitation striking examples remain, proofs, personal testimonies to the desire to maintain the thankful mood in the midst of pain. In such instances praise has not been silenced by the pain.

The sick room or hospital ward where prayer and faith are active show the position in which the Christian sufferer finds himself. He can detect that in union with the Crucified One pain bears fruit in the formation of his own character and nature. He notices this in opposition to all the tendencies and indications to the contrary. He maintains the truth of this in argument against all the forces which would convince him that pain is entirely devastating in its effects on humanity and the world. He is able to make this discovery because it is a matter of his own inspection of his inner self. Such introspection cannot be gainsaid by another. Searching his own self the believing sufferer finds his impregnable fact that pain is productive and can promote his praise of God. That being so he cannot but make a further leap of faith and maintain that what pain does not prevent within his own being it cannot finally destroy outside. While still suffering, he remains believing and praising, and he releases his praise until it covers all created beings. He reminds himself that his own awareness of the fruitfulness of suffering within his own life is confirmed by what he sees in retrospect. That is the mode in which he recognizes the providence of God in his own soul, and he sees reason to infer that in a parallel way he can see the providence of God in the world at large. Looking back he is prepared to point to those demonstrations of suffering which at the time baffled his understanding, but are later recognizable as the occasions for the exercise of divine providence and as real material for human thanksgiving. It was this reflection which upheld Kierkegaard (1813–55), the Danish pessimist who 'from earliest time' had 'been nailed fast to one or another suffering to the verge of insanity.' 'That the heavy suffering is good is something that must be *believed* because it cannot be seen. Perhaps we can see afterwards that it *has been* good, but at the time of suffering we can neither see it, nor, even though ever so many people with the best motives keep on repeating it, can we hear it spoken ; it must be believed.' [8]

Praise from the heart of pain is not yet known to all sufferers, not even to all Christians. The bitterest tragedy in suffering is not its extent, but will continue to be the absence from it of any echo or suggestion of thanksgiving. Seldom will a sufferer ask the ministering priest to read at the bedside *Te Deum laudamus,* 'We praise thee, O God.' For, as was said by Thomas à Kempis (*c.* 1380–1471), 'Jesus has many who love his kingdom in Heaven, but few who bear his Cross,' and 'many love Jesus as long as no hardship touches them.' But 'they who love Jesus for his own sake, and not for the sake of comfort for themselves, bless him in every trial and anguish of heart, no less than in the greatest joy. And were he never willing to bestow comfort on them, they would still always praise him and give him thanks.' [9]

[8] S. Kierkegaard, *Gospel of Suffering,* 1955, p. 32.
[9] *The Imitation of Christ* (tr. by Leo Sherley-Price), Book 2, chap. 11.

E

CHAPTER 5

THE INESTIMABLE LOVE

1

People of faith eagerly speak of God in negative terms. Describing him as immortal, invisible, infinite, incomprehensible, they are employing language which is negative in appearance but deeply positive in intention. Selecting terms which are inextricably interwoven with the limitations and imperfections of human existence in space and time, they mean to strip these away by denying them and so to point to the fullness of reality in the nature and being of God. The negative adjectives are in no sense signals of a negative attitude. It is, for instance, by asserting that God is 'without body, parts or passions' that Article One declares him to be the 'one living and true God, everlasting.' Some way of negation has to be found by man in order to speak of a Creator whose greatness is an 'excellent greatness' and whose peace 'passeth knowledge.' Each negative term is chosen therefore to indicate in what respects God excels and surpasses us.

This manner of speaking of the divine nature is common to Christendom, and it extends to the gifts which are bestowed by the divine bounty. The spiritual inheritance of the Christian is a case in point. 'As divines say of the knowledge of God which we have here, that the negative notion makes up a great part of it, we know rather what he is not than what he is, infinite, incomprehensible, immutable, etc., so it is of this happiness, this inheritance, and indeed it is no other than God,' Archbishop Leighton (1611–84) wrote. Commenting on the description of the Christian's destiny in 1 Peter, chapter 1, verse 4 as 'incorruptible, undefiled, and that fadeth not away,' Leighton singled out this feature : 'We cannot tell you what it is, but we can say so far what it is not, as declares it unspeakably above all the most excellent things of the inferior world and this present life. It is by privatives, by removing imperfections from it, that we describe it, and we can go no further than this.' These negative expressions, then, indicate the limits of our speech. In this they reveal the poverty of our understanding, but they do so by bringing us to the place where language and thinking are silenced by mystery. It is an experience of faith which is noticeably congenial to the English Christian who, avoiding exact and detailed doctrinal definitions and distrustful of exaggeration in his devotions, is a person of restraint in religious expression.

This mood (which is English before it is anglican) accounts in part for the enduring qualities of many religious writings. It lives in the Authorized Version and in the Book of Common Prayer. A supreme statement of it is by Richard Hooker (1554–1600).

> Dangerous it were for the feeble brain of man to wade far into the doings of the Most High ; whom although to know be life, and joy to make mention of his name, yet our soundest knowledge is to know that we know him not as indeed he is, neither can know him ; and our safest eloquence concerning him is our silence, when we confess without confession that his glory is inexplicable, his greatness above our capacity and reach. He is above, and we upon earth ; therefore it behoveth our words to be wary and few.[1]

This paragraph, superbly positive in its wonder, contains a string of negative words and phrases. The negations are themselves marks of the wonder.

2

Our *General Thanksgiving* adds to this vocabulary of won-

[1] R. Hooker, *Ecclesiastical Polity,* Book II, 2.

der. Alongside the more usual negative terms which are
familiar in descriptions of God's eternal being and man's
future bliss we now have 'inestimable.' The word is not one
which has got lodged in literature or conversation as have,
for instance, 'infinite,' 'immortal,' 'invisible.' Many of the
worshippers who repeat it in the *Thanksgiving* scarcely know
of it in any other connection. Like any other word it can be
used loosely in casual conversation, but in more deliberate
settings it is rare and has an aura of mystery.

When children learn this word they remember it, for they
recognize it as coming to them from another world of experience and awe. The adult who says it slowly, as a child
will first do, is immediately under the spell of its influence.
Perhaps the only parallel word at present in use in Christian
worship is the 'inextinguishable' of Charles Wesley's hymn
'O thou who camest from above,' with its petition for the
'flame of sacred love.'

> There let it for thy glory burn
> With inextinguishable blaze,
> And trembling to its source return
> In humble prayer, and fervent praise.

Bishop Reynolds himself seems to have taken special care to
preserve the rarity of this word. Although it occupies so
prominent a place in his *Thanksgiving,* he handled it with
the utmost caution. No instance of his using it is at hand in
his sermons or other writings.

Even when this adjective might have added clarity to his
argument he appears to have avoided it. 'The excellency of
the gospel will appear,' he wrote, 'if we consider the infinite
value and preciousness of the things therein contained,' [2] but
he refrains from describing any of these things as inestimable.
Similarly the adjective is missing from his moving account of
the attributes of God, which offer 'to our view the admirable

[2] *Works,* Vol. V, p. 503.

contexture of justice and mercy, the unspeakable contrivance of redemption and salvation by the gospel.'[3] The omission of the word from passages like these where it could undoubtedly have added to the exposition underlines its significance and importance in the one composition by Edward Reynolds where it does occur. In composing the prayer and giving it its final form Reynolds has employed a word which by its rarity can match thanksgiving for that which is 'above all.' He has saved up this word for this one context, and hesitates to use it in any other. Its rarity remains the secret of its hold on the worshippers who have since repeated it.

'Inestimable' appears in the devotional writings of a contemporary, Thomas Traherne (1637–74). Traherne was himself the author of a book of thanksgivings, which was entitled *A Serious and Pathetical Contemplation of the Mercies of God, in Several Most Devout and Sublime Thanksgivings for the Same*. It has been said of him that 'seldom can there have been a more ardent disciple of thankfulness.'[4] We need not therefore be surprised to find that his use of the word, 'inestimable,' in the context of thanksgiving is illuminating. We may cite three examples from his *Centuries*.

After listing in rhetorical fashion the parts of the body, as God's gifts,—'What diamonds are equal to my eyes; what labyrinths to my ears; what gates of ivory, or ruby leaves, to the double portal of my lips and teeth? Is not sight a jewel? Is not hearing a treasure? Is not speech a glory?'—Traherne continues:

O my Lord pardon my ingratitude, and pity my dullness who am not sensible of these gifts. The freedom of thy bounty hath deceived me. These things were too near to be considered. Thou presentedst me with thy blessings, and I was not aware. But now I give thanks and adore and praise thee for thine inestimable favours.[5]

[3] *Works*, Vol. V, p. 499.
[4] Margaret Willy, *Life was their Cry*, 1950, p. 80.
[5] T. Traherne, *Centuries*, I, 66 (1960 ed., p. 33).

Next, in a description of man's 'highest happiness' :

> When all the world is at peace with us and takes pleasure
> in us, when our actions are delightful, and our persons
> lovely, when our spirits amiable, and our affections ines-
> timable, then are we exalted to the Throne of Glory.[6]

And the final paragraph in this unfinished book contains the
following :

> Our Bridegroom and our King being everywhere, our
> Lover and Defender watchfully governing all worlds, no
> danger or enemy can arise to hurt us, but is immediately
> prevented and suppressed, in all the spaces beyond the
> utmost borders of those unknown habitations which he
> possesseth. Delights of inestimable value are there prepar-
> ing, for everything is present by its own existence.[7]

This richness of language is a strange setting for our adjective
'inestimable,' in comparison with the almost ascetic style of
Edward Reynolds. In the words of H. M. Margolioth the
modern reader can be 'dazzled and delighted by the ardour
and beauty of Traherne's prose.'[8] Nevertheless there is a
similarity in spirit. What is suppressed in corporate worship
may be elaborated at length when private meditations are
being written out. The ease, flow and rapture of Traherne's
writings are implicit in the brevity of Reynolds ; more than
that, they flower from it, as the mental prayers and secret
devotions of Christians can continue to do.

'Inestimable' has become a word whose full meaning may
yet wait to be discovered ; but this discovery is within the
reach of any unnamed Christian. As the Magdalene mur-
mured 'Rabboni' and the doubter Thomas found full ex-

[6] op. cit., IV, 47 (p. 188).
[7] op. cit., V, 10 (p. 228).
[8] op. cit., p. v.

pression for his adoration in 'My Lord and my God,' as the Little Poor Man of Assisi possessed all wealth in repeating throughout the night the divine name, so let each Christian devote a prolonged period of prayer to exclaiming again and again, 'Inestimable love!'

3

The *Oxford English Dictionary* gives two meanings for 'inestimable': (1) 'cannot be reckoned up'; (2) 'priceless.' The former of these will not be applicable in our prayer for it is to be used in the case of collective nouns, as when reference is being made to a number of persons or objects. Where the reference is to a single subject, such as 'love,' the meaning to be accepted is 'priceless.'

The word defies all attempts to find a suitable synonym or equivalent. It cannot even be regarded as the opposite to 'valueless': for 'valuable' implies not only that an object is valued, but also that its value can be or already is known. 'Priceless' states by implication that an object is valued, but that its value either is not yet known or cannot ever be known. It implies uniqueness in its object, which is thus raised both above all accepted standards of comparison and outside every scale of values. A rare word itself, it designates as a first feature in its object unqualified rarity.

The word is not used in the English Old Testament. In the Apocrypha the translators of the Authorized Version use it once (2 Esdras 8 : 21) where the context, recalling the mood of Traherne, is a rich, visionary prayer.

> O Lord, thou that abidest for ever, whose eyes are exalted, and whose chambers are in the air; whose throne is inestimable; whose glory may not be comprehended; . . . hear, O Lord, the prayer of thy servant.

In the New Testament the nearest approach we have to the

word is in Paul's ejaculatory, 'Thanks be to God for his un-speakable gift' (2 Cor. 9 : 15). But although the suggestion [9] has frequently been made that this is the scriptural precedent for 'inestimable' in our prayer, the two adjectives again are far from being identical. That which is 'unspeakable' is un-mentionable or indescribable or, in the specific language of religion, ineffable. To say that it is 'inestimable' is to add the further assertion that it is beyond value as well as speech. The composer of our prayer has provided an adjective which, while allied to these other negative terms which are reserved for statements of the reality of God, crowns them.

The complete clause, 'but above all for thine inestimable love,' demonstrates the primacy of 'inestimable.' Applied to God's love it indicates that the pricelessness not only lifts the love far beyond any attempt to value it, but keeps it entirely outside the reach of any man who would himself attempt to acquire it. The love is a gift. The redemption in which the love is known is a gift. It explains the Pauline contrast between what a man earns and what he is given, his earnings or deservings always being the results of sin and therefore of death and the free gift being eternal life through Jesus Christ our Lord. Love that is priceless is like God's mercy. It can never be bought or won. Therefore this is not only one among all the causes for gratitude : it is to be a crowning cause, 'above all.'

Light is thrown upon this clause by two other passages in the Book of Common Prayer where a similar primacy is being asserted.

The Third Exhortation which the Reformers provided for occasional use 'at the time of the celebration of the Com-munion, the communicants being conveniently placed for the receiving of the Holy Sacrament' had appeared in the 1549 Prayer Book. A noble specimen of religious prose, it is to-day

[9] For example, 'Bishop Reynolds seems to have caught and to have crystallized for all ages of Churchmen the wonderful thought of, 2 Corinthians 9 : 15 : "Thanks be unto God for this unspeakable gift." ' (Dyson Hague, *Through the Prayer Book*, 1948, p. 156.)

unknown to clergy and congregations alike. Its latter section is concerned with the thankful mood of a Christian, and we may class this among the material, along with the prayers to which we have referred, which Bishop Reynolds had available when he composed our *Thanksgiving*. The relationship in phrasing is evident.

> And above all things ye must give most hearty and humble thanks to God, the Father, the Son, and the Holy Ghost, for the redemption of the world by the death and passion of our Saviour Christ, both God and man; who did humble himself, even to the death upon the Cross, for us, miserable sinners, who lay in darkness and the shadow of death; that he might make us the children of God, and exalt us to everlasting life. . . . To him therefore, with the Father and the Holy Ghost, let us give . . . continual thanks; submitting ourselves wholly to his holy will and pleasure, and studying to serve him in true holiness and righteousness all the days of our life.

This statement of the grounds for thanksgiving concentrates entirely upon redemption as wrought by Christ's 'dying for us' and 'the innumerable benefits which by his precious blood-shedding he hath obtained for us.' All the thought is of his Cross. But this limitation of view is understandable from the context. The purpose of the passage is to exhort the communicant to a worthy reception of the sacrament, and as is made clear in the Prayer of Consecration the compilers were in their own minds linking the sacrament specifically with the Cross. Remembrance is made of Jesus Christ who was given to suffer death upon the cross for our redemption.' No mention of the resurrection occurs in the Consecration Prayer. It would have been out of place to mention it in the Exhortation which was written with the communion in view. Thus although the 'above all' of the *General Thanksgiving* is being anticipated, in this case it is restricted to the death of Christ.

Because of this limitation the field of vision in the second of our two passages from the Prayer Book is the more remarkable.

The Proper Preface for Easter Day begins : 'But chiefly are we bound to praise thee for the glorious resurrection of thy Son, Jesus Christ our Lord.'

Worshippers cannot fail to be impressed by the parallel between 'but above all' in the *Thanksgiving* and 'but chiefly' in the Easter Preface. Both are examples of primacy in praise. And when bracketed together, in their amplification of the causes for praise they enrich and deepen each other's interpretation. For the *General Thanksgiving* mentions as the supreme declaration and demonstration of the love of God in Christ Jesus our Lord 'the redemption of the world,' and this (as in the Third Exhortation) is usually taken to be a reference to the death of Christ ; the Easter Preface puts first the resurrection. The Christian who reflects will admit that there need be no contradiction or tension here. We are not thinking of rival events which compete for priority among the causes for giving thanks to God. In fact, the question is at once raised whether we are justified at all in tending to limit the reference in the *Thanksgiving* to the Cross. Conditioned as we are by our necessity to think of one event before the other and of travelling in our mind from one to the other as though each is separate from the other, we easily fall into this limited and limiting view. The Easter Preface can counteract this tendency. The 'chiefly' there refers to the Resurrection following the death upon the Cross. That in itself can lead us to interpret the 'above all' in our prayer as referring to the death upon the Cross followed by the Resurrection. Thus the 'inestimable love' is not to be confined solely to the Cross. It is to be seen both in the death and in the resurrection, for the redemption of the world has been achieved through both. We are here at the heart of a theological debate which has invigorated thinking Christians for generations. It can be summarized by saying that, although on the one hand in the dawn of the first Easter Day there might have seemed no doubt that the resurrection reversed the crucifixion, the second thoughts of even the earliest Christians led them to conclude that the death was itself completed by the resurrection. One Christ is in action in both. One Christ is triumphant in both. The believing Christian can portray *Christus Victor* on the Cross because he can by prayer worship the same victorious Lord in eternity. This assertion of the one, continuous, conquering action of Christ, who 'by his Cross and Passion' and 'by his glorious Resurrection and Ascension' has overcome all our spiritual enemies is at the back of the firm desire to give thanks 'above all' for the 'inestimable love.' The Easter Preface is said or sung on only eight days of the year, but each year during that one week it relights the full faith which can illuminate this phrase for the rest of the year.

Easter emphasis is voiced on the one other occasion when 'inestimable' is used in our Prayer Book, in the Collect appointed for the Second Sunday after Easter. Here again thanksgiving is present, but with a difference. The mood is not one of thanksgiving being expressed but one of thankfulness being asked for. We now approach God who has 'given thine only begotten Son to be unto us both a sacrifice for sin and also an ensample of godly life,' and at first sight our attention appears to be focused again on the crucifixion. But we go on to ask for 'grace that we may always most thankfully receive that his inestimable benefit, and also daily endeavour ourselves to follow the blessed steps of his most holy life.' This petition comes in the Collect for the Second Sunday after Easter. The sacrifice is described as 'his inestimable benefit,' but only within the context of Easter worship. Hence the further petition relating to the worshippers' 'endeavour' to follow Christ's life. The master thought throughout this collect is of the living Christ whose resurrection it is which enables his sacrifice on the Cross to become for us not only a 'benefit,' but also an 'inestimable' one. Again Easter illuminates this rare word. The collect was incorporated in the Prayer Book of 1549. When the *Thanksgiving* by Bishop Reynolds was added in 1661, Eastertide was already established in worshippers' minds as the most fitting season when this adjective is used.

The Christian stands in constant need of the implied reminder that the Jesus of whom he speaks is the Lord whom he worships, 'alive for evermore' (Rev. 1 : 18). His love for that Jesus is not just the respectful reverence which is accorded to some hero or example of the past. It is a response, vibrant and pulsating, a reply alert and quick, to him personally in the now of to-day. Emphasis upon the death of Christ in a Christian's thoughts does not rule out all joy at his resurrection. As Traherne's phrases declare, Jesus is now raised to his 'inestimable throne.' From his death comes 'his inestimable benefit.' His 'inestimable love,' released from the past, is streaming out from eternity into our present and future. Entering human life, suffering, dying, rising again and ascending—through the entire range of his supernatural achievement Jesus accomplishes this. In giving thanks for redemption we are as much praising God for what he has done through his Son our Saviour Jesus Christ in the present and in eternity as in past history. Redemption now is what demonstrates with the greatest immediacy his 'inestimable love,' and only when we are confronted with the Christ of Easter do we fully give thanks for it 'above all.'

4

Thanksgiving for the redemption which has been accomplished in the dying and rising again of Jesus Christ bears the soul rapidly forward to 'the means of grace' and 'the hope of glory.' Both these phrases have their echoes in the writings of Bishop Edward Reynolds, and by turning to these parallels we can enlarge our understanding of what is meant in the prayer.

First, in a notable exhortation Bishop Reynolds urges men to rejoice

> in all the means which he hath appointed to bring men to the knowledge of him, and communion with him. In his ordinances, which are his voice speaking from heaven to us; according to the estimation whereof he accounteth himself regarded by us (Luke 10 : 16). In his ministers, to whom he hath committed the word of reconciliation, whom his people have received as angels of God (Gal. 4 : 14, 15); unto whom what respect, or disrespect is shewed, Christ looketh on as done unto himself (Matthew 10 : 40, 41).[10]

The very fact that this paragraph has none of the neatness of a formal list of 'means' attracts attention. By 'means of grace' the modern worshipper would habitually have himself and his neighbour to understand the sacraments, and he would list these tidily as two or seven. The short passage which we have quoted from Bishop Reynolds knows nothing of this limitation. 'Ordinances' and 'ministers' are both acknowledged to be 'the means' by which God brings us to know him and to be in communion with him, and there is no suggestion that in this connection 'ministers' are to be regarded solely as dispensers of the sacraments. To them 'he hath committed the word of reconciliation.' The reference is to preaching and, by implication, to the reconciling influence of the minister in all pastoral work and responsibility.

And there is a ministry of the laity no less than of the clergy. All are called to be God's workmen. This ancient truth of scripture is stirring to life again during the twentieth century, bringing with it a generosity of outreach and a warmth of devotion which break through the surface of the habits of a lifetime as spring flowers push up through the soil and invest the scene with colour and vitality.

[10] *Works,* Vol. IV, pp. 399–400.

Indeed, recognition of any means of grace carries with it the readiness to recognize others without number. The scriptures raise literature to a new status of seriousness and beauty. The water, the bread and the wine give to every meal a new depth of fellowship and sacrifice. The ordination of ministers goes hand in hand with vocations for mankind at large. And the houses of God in the land are not only the places of worship, but also homes, factories, shops, hospitals, schools, prisons, institutions. There is no foreseeable limit to the scope of the creative and redemptive love which can take people and places and things and make of them additional means of grace.

'The means of grace' is a phrase which is capable of being expanded afresh in each new situation. During the present century Christians of all communions are involved in the tensions, misunderstandings and advances of ecumenical co-operation, and in connection with this striving towards unity amongst Christians manifestoes and memoranda will continue to multiply. Each new formula tends to take the place of what has gone before. This process reveals the need for a parent-phrase which can produce new insights and can itself live on. 'The means of grace' may be taken as a phrase of this nature. As long as it is preserved from becoming the sole property of committees who draft documents and is treasured by the worshipping community of Christians, it is likely to remain as a centre of unifying experience. To this end it must be guarded, loved and repeated in the continuous experience of worship. Its inclusion in the *General Thanksgiving,* a prayer of anglican origin but shared in actual use by different traditions, can contribute to this result.

This cannot be far from the mind of the Christian worshipper as he continues to use this phrase. In so doing he recalls those particular means of grace, of whatever number, which he himself recognizes and personally receives. His reaction to these means is gratitude, for that is his response to grace itself. This reaction or response he shares with all other

Christians, pointing to an underlying unity in personal discipleship which is already present.

For there is a mysterious interconnection between grace and gratitude which appears to pervade all stages in the Christian life. This originates in the New Testament. It has been forcibly summarized by a recent New Testament scholar, who maintains that in some passages the word *charis* or 'grace' is even used to indicate 'the gratitude elicited by a gracious act' (Luke 6 : 32-4) or 'an act done by a Christian that is pleasing to God, as in 1 Peter 2 : 19f., where it is said that to suffer wrongfully for conscience' sake is *charis*.' Thus 'grace' or 'thanksgiving' may describe the Christian's motive of service to God : as in Hebrews 12 : 28, 'Let us have grace whereby we may serve God acceptably with reverence and godly fear' (A.V.), or 'let us therefore give thanks to God, and so worship him as he would be worshipped, with reverence and awe' (N.E.B.). Again, 2 Cor. 4 : 15 has 'all things are for your sakes, that the abundant grace might through the thanksgiving of many redound to the glory of God' (A.V.), or 'it is for your sake that all things are ordered, so that, as the abounding grace of God is shared by more and more, the greater may be the chorus of thanksgiving that ascends to the glory of God' (N.E.B.). Here are Christian insights before they have become systematized. The close conjunction of 'grace' and 'thanksgiving' in such a way that the distinction between them is at times almost impossible to draw shows how inseparable they are as elements in the mature Christian life.

This is the point which Canon Richardson stresses. 'Thanksgiving to God for his inexpressible gift in Christ (2 Cor. 9 : 15) is the mainspring of Christian conduct and the key-category of Christian ethics. The whole Christian life is response to the gift of God (Rom. 5 : 15-17; Ephes. 2 : 8; 3 : 7; 4 : 7; 1 Peter 4 : 10); it is response to the grace of our Lord Jesus Christ, by which he became poor, though he was rich (2 Cor. 8 : 1-9); Christians give themselves in thanksgiving to God (2 Cor. 8 : 5); they live in a state of grace, empowered by the grace of thanksgiving to perform their good works (cf. Acts 6 : 8 ; 13 : 43 ; Rom. 5 : 2 ; Col. 3 : 16f. ; 2 Tim. 2 : 1 ; Heb. 13 : 9, etc.).'[11]

This chain of texts which are decisive in our interpretation of the New Testament writings demonstrates that a phrase which is at the centre of our *Thanksgiving* corresponds to an experience at the heart of every Christian's life.

Next, we have the comments of Bishop Edward Reynolds on the words, 'the hope of glory.' After quoting the words as a sub-heading in a sermon, he continues :

> The spirit of adoption is even now a glorious thing 'but it doth not yet appear what we shall be'; only this he hath assured us of, that we shall be 'like unto him,' shall 'see him as he is,' shall 'appear with him in glory,' shall 'sit upon his throne,' and 'be ever with him' (1 John 3 : 1, 2 ; Col. 3 : 4). And this blessed hope, secured by the witness of the Spirit (who is the seal and earnest of our eternal inheritance) filleth the hearts of believers with 'joy unspeakable and full of glory' ; while they look not on the things that are seen, but on the things that are not seen.[12]

'Even now'—this in the mind of the composer of our *Thanksgiving* is the unmistakable mark of Christian hope. According to him our hope is firmly planted in the present. That for which we hope is in the future—beyond our grasp, beyond our sight, beyond the grave ; but our hope itself is an attitude or disposition or way of looking at things which is being experienced and shared now. Any attempt to analyse the nature of Christian hope must include among its ingredients trust, expectation, patience, certainty ; but these are all to be found among the day-to-day qualities of Christians now. The more we are aware of the future reality of that for which we hope, the more we are conscious of the actual present reality

[11] Alan Richardson, *An Introduction to the Theology of the New Testament*, 1958, pp. 282–3.
[12] *Works*, Vol. IV, p. 401.

of our hoping. And it is because hope is thus discovered and preserved in the ever-present now of this life and is already our possession that we can give thanks for it.

In mentioning hope among the grounds for our gratitude to God we need to observe this distinction between the object of hope and hope itself. True enough the term 'hope' can be applied to the object, as when the man of religion says that God is his hope, but this is a secondary use of the term. It is more natural to exclaim with the psalmist, 'And now, Lord, what is my hope : truly my hope is even in thee' (Ps. 39 : 8). God, Christ, the Church can only be called our hope because in the first place we put our hope *in* them. So, too, in giving thanks for 'the hope of glory' we do not have in mind solely or even primarily that promised hereafter whose circumstances we cannot visualize and whose nature we cannot imagine. We are primarily expressing thankfulness for the joyful expectation and confident serenity which are already ours. We do not yet possess the glory, but we do possess the hope ; and it is for the hope that we give thanks.

This is made possible by the special quality of hope as possessed by a Christian in vivid contrast to other moods which have been given the name. The addition of a new section on Hope to the proposed Revised Catechism (1962) draws attention to its importance in a modern Christian's life.

Christian hope is different from the unsettlement of the searcher or the struggle of an intellectual agnostic who speaks of hope with a falter. Thus, in 'We are of those' by Christina Rossetti (1830–94)

> We are of those who tremble at thy word,
> Who faltering walk in darkness towards our close
> Of mortal life, by terrors curbed and spurred—
>   We are of those.
>
> Not ours the heart thy loftiest love hath stirred,
> Not such as we thy lily and thy rose,
> Yet, Hope of those who hope with hope deferred,
>   We are of those.

F

From the same writer comes

> My faith burns low, my hope burns low,
> Only my heart's desire cries out in me,
> By the deep thunder of its want and woe
> Cries out to thee.

Christian hope, on the other hand, is to be distinguished from the warm, unthinking, effervescent mood of the born optimist. Discussing the appropriateness of the expression, 'a sneaking hope,' a leader writer in *The Times* drew in bold outline the contours of this more popular form of hope. 'Hope at its strongest is a buoyant, surging thing, leaping up as the heart does on beholding a rainbow in the sky, but, even when continual deferment reduces it to the wan and pensive image as visualized by Watts, hope remains hope and it is to this somewhat depressed version of the emotion that the despised word can join itself without fearing rebuff.' He continues

> The sneaking hope does not set its sights high and is modest in its ambitions, sometimes doing no more than to keep its fingers crossed. What is more, it carries its diffidence to the length of doubting whether the object of its desire is itself legitimate.[13]

This portrait of hope is far removed from the Christian account of it. In short, 'the hope of which we speak is something different from what men usually mean when they speak of hope. In common speech "hope" means a strong desire for something which may be possible but is not certain. What is spoken of here is something that we wait for expectantly and yet patiently, because we know that it can never disappoint us.'[14]

[13] *The Times*, July 9th, 1960.
[14] *Christ—the Hope of the World*, World Council of Churches, 1954, p. 6.

The Inestimable Love

The ecumenical report from which this statement is taken further amplifies the background of what a Christian means by hope. 'We have this confidence because our hope is based upon what we know of God, and because we know of him through what he has done. Our hope is not the projection of our desires upon an unknown future, but the product in us of God's acts in history, and above all of his act in raising Jesus Christ from the dead.' These two sentences clarify considerably the nature of Christian hope. That our hope is founded and built upon divine revelation and is the result of our knowledge of what God has already done among mankind removes it from the haze of sentimentality or emotion in which it tends to get lost. Modern man has to learn how to nurture a longing without confusing it with wistfulness. The assurance that Christian hope is in no sense a 'projection of our desires upon an unknown future' will assist in this. But what is most striking from the point of view of our own present enquiry is that this quotation cannot refrain from using in this connection the phrase 'above all' and from applying this to God's act in the resurrection of Jesus Christ. This is a remarkable echo, from an independent source, of the 'above all' which in our *Thanksgiving* is related to the 'inestimable love' in redemption; and here the 'above all' is explicitly that of Easter.

The hope, therefore, no less than the 'inestimable love in the redemption of the world,' no less than 'the means of grace,' is dependent upon the resurrection of Jesus Christ. 'If in this life only we have hope in Christ, we are of all men most miserable' (1 Cor. 15 : 19). 'Blessed be the God and Father of our Lord Jesus Christ' who 'hath begotten us again unto a lively hope through the resurrection of Jesus Christ from the dead' (1 Peter 1 : 3). And just as the event of the resurrection created the new situation of hope, so the experience of the risen Christ extends that hope into the lives of Christians of each succeeding generation. For all it is a matter of 'Christ in you, the hope of glory' (Col. 1 : 27).

This characteristic of the Christian's hope as an experience or an attitude which is always available follows from its integral connection with Christ's resurrection. But it finds expression in more general terms which are in varying degrees corollaries of that. Proverbial sayings such as 'hoping against hope' or 'where there's life, there's hope' are related to it. Most dramatic of all is the symbolic description of hope as an anchor, which is familiar to great numbers of people who would be surprised to learn of its biblical origin. Hebrews 6 : 19 intends this to be a spiritual symbol, referring to hope as 'the anchor of the soul.' But the stress upon hope as a present experience remains definite. The main detail in the symbolism appears to be that the promise for which we hope is like an anchor out of sight. A ship is tossed on the surface of the water, but its cable is attached to a hidden anchor and holds it secure ; so the soul has to encounter storms on the surface of life, but hope fixes it to the unseen hereafter and keeps it safe.

If we have rightly interpreted the thoughts of our author, the dominant theme throughout this central section of *A general Thanksgiving* is that of the resurrection of Christ. Without the resurrection there would be no grounds for giving thanks for redemption, for means of grace or for hope. With the resurrection there is no reason for refusing to. But where the resurrection of Christ is acknowledged, the risen Christ himself is known to be at hand. 'Thine inestimable love' is pre-eminently the love of Christ. The means of grace are inseparable from 'the grace of our Lord Jesus Christ.' 'The hope of glory' is 'Christ in you.' This section of the *Thanksgiving* has not been fully offered until it has been uplifted and ennobled by the worshipper's sublime awareness of the presence of the risen Lord. Christ's resurrection was from the beginning the first item in the Church's gospel : it remains 'above all' the reason for the Church's praise.

According to the Christian hope glory which is now hidden will be openly revealed at 'the end of the Age' (R.S.V.). This manifestation will be inaugurated by the second coming of Christ. 'And he shall come again with glory to judge both the quick and the dead.' 'The Son of man shall come in the glory of his Father with his angels' (Matthew 16 : 27). 'They shall see the Son of man coming with power and great glory' (Matthew 24 : 30). The certainty within our hope is therefore not that we are approaching glory but that glory is approaching us. Twentieth century man is being driven to accept this hope by the collapse of all his lesser hopes. The despairs and disillusions which have become the common feature of human affairs following the nineteenth century optimisms prepare the way for this.

Dr. Alec Vidler has written :

The last truth about our individual achievements in this age, however excellent and worthwhile they may have been, is that in the end we have to acknowledge there is nothing more that we can do. The tide of life is running out. Our earthly habitation is failing us. We are helpless, and our only hope lies in having something done to us. Thus at last we may each be brought to say with the Spirit and the bride of the Apocalypse : 'Come ; even so, come, Lord Jesus.' Likewise, the last truth about the whole human race may be that at the end of all its finest experiments and achievements in civilization it will be confronted by the spectacle of universal failure and disaster, and will have to confess that it is helpless and can do no more, that its only hope lies in having something done to it. So the history of this world will close like the Bible with the cry : 'Come, Lord, Jesus.' And then he will come in power and great glory.[15]

Unreservedly the Christian can accept this as valid material for thanksgiving. He is in fact in a stronger position to-day to offer thanks on this account than in any of his predecessors.

[15] A. R. Vidler, *Christian Belief and this World*, 1956, p. 53.

The higher the scrap-heaps of abandoned hopes around us, the firmer will be our thankfulness for that hope which is the ultimate survivor of the rest. 'The God of all grace' has called us 'unto his eternal glory by Christ Jesus.' With that glory in view he will 'perfect' or 'restore' (N.E.B.), 'stablish, strengthen, settle' all who in hope now suffer 'a while' (1 Peter 5 : 10). And the sufferings of this present world are not comparable to that glory ahead which is awaited by all 'in hope' (Rom. 8 : 18f.). Therefore, in the fine words of the Prayer Book Office for the Burial of the Dead, the whole of a Christian's life can be lived 'in sure and certain hope of the resurrection to eternal life through our Lord Jesus Christ.'

Grace and glory together embrace the whole stretch of man's existence. Grace is the application of God's 'inestimable love' to man in this life, glory the application of the same love to man in the next. Grace is redemption at work upon man while he is on the road, *in via,* glory is redemption enjoyed by man when he has reached home, *in patria.* There is no circumstance or situation of man which can remove a Christian outside the combined scope of these two activities of the divine love. He is uninterruptedly within the range of grace and glory. We have a parallel in the wording of the traditional marriage vows. 'For better, for worse, for richer, for poorer, in sickness and in health'—the Christian husband and wife take each other for life by taking each other for these. It is not possible to imagine any eventuality which is not covered by the actual vows. Similarly, the Christian soul has been taken by God for life by being taken for grace and for glory. It is not possible to suggest any setting in this life or the next which is not covered by the love which is designated by these two words. The Christian's strivings are the prelude to his destiny. All is the achievement of the 'inestimable love,' and the abiding promise to each soul now is

> Thou shalt see my glory soon,
> When the work of grace is done.

CHAPTER 6

A DUE SENSE

1

When Jesus rode into Jerusalem he did not choose as his mount a proud, white, royal charger, but an ass; and when the crowds surged round to welcome him they had neither pageantry nor ceremonial. The welcome was improvised. Whatever came handy was used to wave. Tree branches were torn down. Clothes were laid not only on the ass but also across the route. This rough and ready arrangement was, according to Matthew, completed by the children joining in.

In Matthew's account the incident of the children is emphasized. 'The children' were still 'crying in the temple' and echoing hosanna even after Jesus had entered the building and emptied it of 'all them that sold and bought in the temple.' This prolonged shouting of the children called for explanation. In answer to the question, 'Hearest thou what these say?,' he replied, 'Yea; have ye never read, "Out of the mouths of babes and sucklings thou hast perfected praise"' (Matthew 21 : 16–17).

Psalm 8, verse 2, which Jesus is here said to be quoting, has

Out of the mouth of very babes and sucklings hast thou ordained strength.[1]

The version quoted in the Gospel is that of the Septuagint, or Greek translation of the Old Testament. Christian devotion has recognized in this alteration of the wording a significant statement of God's ways. Matthew Henry's comment

---

[1] In this form the psalm provides the opening of the Prayer Book Collect for the Innocents' Day.

is enlightening. 'Christ is so far from being ashamed of the services of little children, that he takes particular notice of them (and children love to be taken notice of), and is well pleased with them. If God may be honoured by babes and sucklings, who are made to hope at the best, much more by children who are grown up to maturity and some capacity.' Further, 'praise is perfected out of the mouth of such; it has a peculiar tendency to the honour and glory of God for little children to join in his praises; the praise would be accounted defective and imperfect if they had not their share in it.' But, finally, 'God *perfecteth praise,* by *ordaining strength out of the mouths of babes and sucklings.* When great things are brought about by weak and unlikely instruments, God is thereby much honoured, for his strength is *perfected in weakness,* and the infirmities of the babes and sucklings serve for a foil to the divine power.'

In this interpretation of the episode the Christian moves beyond the literal meaning of the words. Here, as in other scriptural contexts, he notices an affinity between 'children' and 'Christians.' Those who follow Christ are to become as little children. The children of God, the children of light, successors of the children of Israel, include grown men and women. Disciples of any age take 'children' to mean not alone patterns and examples, but also themselves.

But if we are to be identified in this way as 'the little children' of the God and Father of our Lord Jesus Christ, we are called to become as such on more than one occasion. Our Lord's well remembered remark mentions entry into the kingdom of heaven. A similar disposition is necessary, as a renewal of that entry, each time we enter an act of worship. This is to be the constant spiritual setting of every act of Christian prayer, and it applies to our thanksgiving. All our hymns are 'children's hymns.' *Ex ore infantium,* meaning literally 'out of the mouth of those that cannot speak,' is the motto of the praises of inarticulate men if these are to be 'perfected.'

A Due Sense

2

This distinctively Christian requirement can be detected behind the petition, 'And, we beseech thee, give us that due sense of all thy mercies.' It is the only petition in *A general Thanksgiving,* a fact which heightens its importance. The phrase is followed by the words, 'that our hearts may be unfeignedly thankful, and that we shew forth thy praise,' but these clauses are only additional in the sense that they amplify the meaning of the main request. The 'due sense' for which we ask is to have specific results, producing in us unfeignedly thankful hearts and the shewing forth of God's praise. These therefore are spiritual consequences in the lives of Christians, dependent upon whether in the first place there is a 'due sense' of all God's mercies.

The expression, made familiar by regular use, has been dulled by repetition. We assume without conscious thought that 'due sense' can only mean one thing. It is, we say, that sense of God's mercies which is due to him. Having accepted by implication that definition we have not paused to consider whether, if this be the 'sense' of all God's mercies for which we ask, we can ever expect to attain it. There have doubtless been Christians in every generation who have taken as their aim 'the habitual living . . . in a sense of the presence, the power, the prevenience of God, the healing Divine Dwarfer of our poor little man-centred, indeed even self-centred, schemes' [2]; but 'a sense of the presence' of God is not to be confused with a trustful and happy mood of ignorance of what all his mercies are. When a man's active, but finite, mind attempts to list the infinite expressions of divine loving kindness, he is turned in on his own incapacities. We are back with Hooker and his description of silence as our safest eloquence. Human thought falters. Human speech fails. 'Who can express the noble acts of the Lord : or shew forth

[2] *Letters from Baron Friedrich von Hügel to a Niece,* ed. G. Greene, 1928, pp. 20–1.

all his praise?' (Ps. 106 : 2). 'I know and confess,' à Kempis prayed, 'that I am wholly unable to render You proper thanks, even for the least of the many blessings that You grant me, for I am less than the least of Your gifts. When I consider Your boundless generosity, my spirit grows faint at its greatness.' [3] We have no 'due sense' which can match both the majesty and the mercy of God.

Are we then in this petition asking the impossible? Not if we are prepared to make one vital distinction. On the one hand a 'sense of God's mercies' can be called a 'due sense' because it is one which is said to be 'due' to God; on the other hand, it may be a 'due sense' because it is that sense of God's mercies which is 'due' from man. It is in the second respect that we are able to use the expression.

We are confronted with the entire, vast, exhilarating and dazzling panorama of a universe which is devoted to giving praises to its Creator God. Our gaze can travel up and down the numberless orders in this created universe. Our ears can hear again and again the recital of their praises as recorded in the psalms and the spiritual hymns of our Christian heritage. These praises, in varying stages and degrees of wonder, correspond to similarly graded conditions of awareness of the divine mercies which call them forth. Angels, planets, men, dumb beasts, insects, plants, stones, praise differently. The sense of God's mercies will differ according to the praises of which each grade is capable. If men can develop a greater sense of these mercies than do animals, this again will be different from that of angels. The sense of all his mercies which is 'due' from us is that which God knows is possible for us to offer. It is neither higher nor lower than our capacities.

If from one aspect this is to state a limitation upon what man's offering to God can be, it is also from another aspect to enlarge man's responsibility. The sense of God's mercies which is 'due' from him is that which exalts him. He is nature's spokesman, nature's priest. The praises which are

[3] *The Imitation of Christ,* Book 2, Chapter 22.

due from him are to represent elements in the world which have no voice other than his.

This conception, enriching our interpretation of the 'due sense' of God's mercies, recurs in Christian literature. We may cite one unsurpassed example from anglican thought. 'As it is the duty of such creatures as he hath fitted for it to render praise to him,' Robert Leighton wrote, 'so it is their happiness. All created things, indeed, declare and speak his glory : the heavens sound it forth, and the earth and sea resound and echo it back. But his reasonable creatures hath he peculiarly framed, both to take notice of his glory in all the rest, and to return it from and for all the rest, in a more express and lively way.' Archbishop Leighton continues :

> In this lower world, it is man alone that is made capable of observing the glory of God, and of offering him praises. He expresses it well, who calls man 'the world's high priest' : all the creatures bring their oblations of praise to him, to offer up for them and for himself, for whose use and comfort they are made. The light and motion of the heavens, and all the variety of creatures below them, speak this to man—He that made us and you, and made us for you, is great, and wise, and worthy to be praised. And you are better able to say this than we ; therefore praise him on our behalf, and on your own. Oh! he is great and mighty, he is the Lord our Maker.[4]

Man may not abdicate from this priestly status, in spite of the efforts of poets to coax him. No part of nature, under the control of natural law or instinct, can perform the task for him. So John Keats (1795–1821) was denying both the Creator's power and man's role when in 'Bright Star' he wrote of

> The moving waters at their priestlike task
> Of pure ablution round earth's human shores.

[4] Robert Leighton, *A Practical Commentary upon the First Epistle of Saint Peter* (on 1 Peter 5 : 11).

Christians can allow those lines to be beautiful, but not true.

Nor has man's priestly role been cancelled by scientific speculation or by interplanetary or outer spatial exploration. His function remains as that of a spokesman of the created world, regardless of the range or magnificence of it. It is derived from his power of speech. It raises him above his fellows in creation. Nevertheless this is his limited dignity for it subordinates him to God, and his power of speech is a restricted one. Our thoughts and ways are not God's.

In the Christian outlook upon the universe it is the humility of man's thanksgivings and praises which is their distinctive note. For that reason, when we ask for 'that due sense,' our strict intention is to ask only for that limited sense of the divine bounty which mercifully is required of ourselves. No matter what be the heights of wonder to which the soul climbs in meditation upon 'creation, preservation, and all the blessings of this life . . . and above all, . . . redemption,' we are not asking for the crystal clarity of vision which is associated with angelic acts of adoration nor for any exceptional ecstasy of love such as has been claimed by certain mystics. Only that 'sense of all' God's 'mercies' of which man is capable is being begged. This must be proportionate to man's capacities. It must be relevant to the general state of man without being the prize of favoured or gifted individuals. It can only mean and be one thing. It is that 'sense' of God's goodness which issues in service. The petition is offered in the mood of John Keble.

> We need not wind ourselves too high
> For mortal man beneath the sky

—even though 'new every morning is the love.' [5]

The subordination of man to God, the abandonment of man to the worship of God, and his acceptance of the fact

[5] *English Hymnal* 260 and *Songs of Praise* 31, verse 5. This verse is omitted from *Hymns Ancient and Modern*.

that his fullest expression of his sense of the wonder and love of God as far as this life is concerned lies in his own self-application to a life of service have been massively summarized in the classic volume of Bishop K. E. Kirk. Although the theme throughout his study is that the *summum bonum,* the highest good, of man is to be located in the vision of God as the end of all human life, still he made this remarkable reservation as regards the practice or attainment of that end.

'The doctrine that the "end of man is the vision of God," as a practical maxim for life, implies that the Christian should set himself first of all to focus his thought upon God in the spirit of worship. It implies this of necessity, and of necessity it implies nothing more—nothing whatever as to the achieving of pleasures, rapture, exaltation in the act of worship. The only achievement man has the right to hope for is that of greater Christian saintliness—greater zeal for service—coming from this direction of the heart and mind to God.' This, Kirk contended, meant 'to look towards God, and from that "look" to acquire insight both into the follies of one's own heart and the needs of one's neighbours, with power to correct the one no less than to serve the other.' [6]

It would be a hard task to search for a more telling outline of thoughts which underlie the phrase 'due sense of all thy mercies' and the clauses which follow.

3

What is vital in the frequent use of *A general Thanksgiving* is that these limitations which are inherent in man's present condition and in his status as creature shall be frankly and humbly accepted. There is a reason why this petition comes at the end of the prayer.

A due sense of God's mercies is being asked for and has to be asked for because man in his self-centredness and littleness

[6] K. E. Kirk, *The Vision of God,* 1931, p. 444f.

of outlook is continually forgetting them. His nature and
circumstances are such that only as a result of a deliberate
move on his part and as an expression of an inner cultivated
steadfastness can he be expected to maintain, in the words of
John Henry Newman (1801–90), 'a habit of affectionate
musing upon God's providence towards him in times past, and
of overflowing thankfulness for them'[7] or 'the temper of
dependence upon God's providence, and thankfulness under
it, and careful memory of all he has done for us.' Newman's
exhortation to this end is pertinent.

> It would be well if we were in the habit of looking at all
> we have, as God's gift, undeservedly given, and day by day
> continued to us solely by his mercy. He gave; he may take
> away. He gave us all we have, life, health, reason, enjoy-
> ment, the light of conscience; whatever we have good and
> holy within us; whatever faith we have; whatever of a
> renewed will; whatever love towards him; whatever power
> over ourselves; whatever prospect of heaven. He gave us
> relatives, friends, education, training, knowledge, the Bible,
> the Church. All comes from him. He gave; he may take
> away. . . . While he continues his blessings, we should
> follow David and Jacob, by living in constant praise and
> thanksgiving, and in offering up to him of his own.[8]

The emphasis on habit and on its earnest cultivation is what
in this extract most nearly approximates to the theme of the
'due sense' being asked for.

But Newman adds an observation which may in part indicate a reason for the additional urgency of this need among
modern people. Although preaching a hundred years ago, his
words are by no means outdated. He points out that the thankful man has to be a person of a certain type. His character
is that of 'a gentle, tender, affectionate, timid mind—easily

[7] J. H. Newman, *Parochial Sermons*, 1842, Vol. V, p. 88.
[8] op. cit., p. 95.

frightened, easily agitated, loving God so much that he fears to lose him, and, like St. Thomas perhaps, anxious for sight and possession from earnest desire of having them.' Further, men and women of this type 'are easily downcast, and must be treated kindly; they soon despond, they shrink from the world, for they feel its rudeness, which bolder natures do not.'[9] The happiness of 'a child-like, sensitive, sweet mind' is bound to lie in tracing lovingly, and gratefully acknowledging, what has been given in the past. It is built on the past 'experience of God's mercies.'[10]

If there is an element of exaggeration in this account of the thankful man that may be because it is the preacher's own self-portrait. But even when we have made allowances to that extent we cannot but acknowledge that this thankful man by no means resembles what would now pass as the portrait of a twentieth century man. Modern conditions do not by and large produce the 'child-like, sensitive, sweet mind,' and modern natures are on the whole the 'bolder natures' themselves. Therefore, if man in any age has not found it easy to maintain a mind of thankfulness to God, contemporary man will experience even greater difficulty in this. He, more than most, will need to ask for a sense of God's mercies.

But the fault is not only in our surroundings or inherited tendencies. These have infected the Church, whose worship has not been without blame in this respect.

The earliest Christian forms of worship which have survived vibrate with praise. The present-day worshipper who only knows those forms of worship which he uses in his own Church is not likely to appreciate how thin and impoverished our Christian approach to God has become. Changes have been demanded and alterations made from motives which at the time may have been justifiable and totally honourable. The desire for simplification, a determination to protest against and resist superstitious additions, the simple cult of

[9] op. cit., p. 91.
[10] op. cit., p. 92.

Englishness, the necessity to shorten services and save time—such are some of the factors which have resulted in a loss of colour and of joy. 'Under the dull skies of England we hardly realize a thought which is bright with the sunshine of the glorious East of Palestine and Greece. The old Latin service books were formed in times of deep despondency, when it seemed as much as man could do to keep alive any sort of Christianity at all : and though we removed much of their excessive sadness at the Reformation, we are still strangers to the triumphant hope and overflowing thankfulness which runs through the prayers of the Eastern Church. We have but a sample of it in our noble closing hymn, "Glory be to God on high" ; and that was never written in the sombre West. Its echoes come down to us from the last prayer of Polycarp himself, before the fire was lighted at his feet.' [11] The enrichment of worship, including the re-statement of thanksgiving with praise and adoration, has proved to be one of the strongest influences behind efforts at Prayer Book revision. At the age of ninety-two L. P. Jacks (1860–1955) observed that this was the direction of his own long, honest, intellectual and spiritual pilgrimage : 'The little I now profess to know about God has the effect of making my religion predominantly an affair of gratitude. Had I the making of a new liturgy, it would be framed throughout in terms of thanksgiving.' [12]

But the fervour of 'eucharistic' moods is not attributable solely to eastern exuberance. Speaking of the Christian Church as a whole, Heiler, who was successively Roman Catholic, Evangelical and Lutheran, remarked that in the worship of the early Christians praise and thanksgiving normally occupied a much larger place than in the later liturgies. He candidly gave his explanation. 'When enthusiasm had passed away and the assurance of salvation had become weaker, the prayer for salvation took the prominent place.' [13]

There is a parallel between this shift of emphasis in the

[11] H. M. Gwatkin, *The Sacrifice of Thankfulness*, 1917, pp. 137–8.
[12] L. P. Jacks, *Near the Brink. Observations of a Nonagenarian*, 1952, p. 23.   [13] F. Heiler, *Prayer*, Eng. tr., 1932, p. 318.

worship of the Church and what occurs in the experience of the Christian. The development of the later liturgies has been on the whole towards a diminution of gratitude. So too the personal histories of Christians after their youthful days of 'enthusiasm,' conversion, confirmation, the 'first communion,' have very often gone in the same direction. We are led to one conclusion. Effort is required of a man if he is to maintain and eventually increase his sense of God's mercies; but the effort needs the assistance of grace. Thus the petition for 'that due sense' of the mercies leads us full circle. It will result in a life of service. It can also result in a renewal of gratitude, for gratitude to God for his mercies fades unless unfailing prayer is offered for a due sense of what those mercies are.

CHAPTER 7

ACTION

1

In spite of the brilliance with which thankfulness shines into and through the whole arena of Christian living, the conclusion of our *Thanksgiving* comes to many as an anticlimax.

After the recital of the acts of God in creation and redemption, after recalling not only 'all the blessings of this life' but also and 'above all' God's 'inestimable love,' one might have expected to have been carried on and upward to the end of this thanksgiving prayer by a rhythm of increasing intensity, mounting to some superb culmination in which would be enumerated still further glories and wonders. In a Bach fugue each voice enters in turn only to return together in majestic splendour, restating in harmony or powerful unison, and with magnificent richness, as a climax to the whole work its original or central theme.

> The great pedal dominant
> Gathers into one
> All wanderers, all lost,
> All the undone :
> Plunges to the keynote,
> They following him come
> To his burning finality,
> His absolute home.[1]

No final flourish or recapitulation of this kind occurs in *A general Thanksgiving*. It is not even rounded off, as some

[1] Hal Summers, *A Fugue in Saint Margaret's*, 1961.

might choose, with 'Hallelujah' or 'Gloria.' No hint of heroics is here. Instead, we are presented with a plain petition that thankfulness may be real—'that our hearts may be un-feignedly thankful'—and that the praise which is being spoken may be 'shewn forth' in lives as well as with lips. In these subdued tones the prayer closes, emphasizing behaviour. And this apparent preoccupation with a Christian's conduct, coming as the conclusion to an act of thanksgiving, is ambiguous.

The implication might be that 'lives' are to supplant 'lips,' or that the showing forth of God's praise with our mouths will sooner or later be found not necessary. According to this interpretation the one requirement is to remove thanksgiving from speech to action.

This was not the view of the writer of our prayer.

In his remarkable series of Seven Sermons on the Four-teenth Chapter of Hosea Bishop Reynolds gave special promi-nence to a phrase in verse 2 : 'So will we render the calves of our lips.' 'Calves' he took to mean 'sacrifices,' and continued : 'Now thanksgiving is . . . called the "calves," or sacrifices "of the lips," to intimate, that, after all God's mercies upon us in pardoning our sins, and in multiplying his grace and spiritual comforts upon us,—we, like beggars, have nothing to return, but the bare acknowledgements and praises of our lips, words for wonders : and those words too his own gifts : we cannot render them to him, before we have received them from him.' [2] Reynolds leaves no doubt about his convictions in the matter. 'Words for wonders' are man's proper response. Therefore, in worship the mouth is as necessary as the heart. True enough that spoken worship may be empty, if it is neither accom-panied nor occasioned by worship in the heart. But when the heart is full, praises must be uttered. Thanksgiving is to be felt. Thanksgiving is to be lived. But it is also to be spoken.

[2] *Works,* Vol. III, p. 219.

2

This linking of lips with lives in one act of self-dedication is an expression of the primitive urge to bind body with mind in religious experience. The urge has persisted throughout man's pilgrimage. Even the savage rituals which to the modern observer have more the appearance of crudity than of sincerity testify to the same drive. Praise to the Creator-God has inspired particularly the ritual dance, and instances of this are recorded in the Old Testament.

The same desire to keep mind and body in unison reappears in the basic Christian insistence upon a worshipper's offering being a presentation of his whole personality. When, for example, Paul exhorts the Christians at Rome 'that ye present your bodies a living sacrifice, holy, acceptable to God, which is your reasonable service,' he immediately proceeds to emphasize 'the renewing of your mind' by means of which the dedicating Christians are to be 'transformed' (Rom. 12 : 1, 2). Mind and body are to be partners in the Christian religion.

Providentially Christians have preserved the catalogue of praises in Psalm 150. This song survives as a monumental example of man's struggle to achieve the entire offering of himself in an act of thanksgiving. The six stanzas, reverberating with force and fervour, make our phrase, 'not only with our lips, but in our lives,' look pale ; and they can provide a great deal of the meaning to be conveyed by it. To cite one of its most colourful phrases, 'Praise him in the cymbals and dances' has not been deleted from Christian psalmody ; and this in itself draws attention to the demand for bodily expression of praise.

The Christian religion is able to appeal to such passages of scripture in defence of its reluctance to eradicate from its forms of worship observances which may be traced back to the most primitive expressions of faith and dedication. What is being symbolized, however imperfectly, in the ceremonial dance of African and eastern tribal religions includes the offering, in joyful self-dedication, of the entire personality—of body as well as of mind and spirit; and it is in order to preserve that offering in its fullness and to complete it that the Christian Church is committed to retaining in one form or another bodily actions in worship which have their origin in the dance.

Dr. Austin Farrer has summarized the distinction between its roles in the Christian and non-Christian religions. In the non-Christian environment the dance is everything. It is not merely the symbol of a spiritual reality or experience; it is identical with it. Christians, on the other hand, avoid taking the symbol for that which is symbolized. They do not 'take rhythm to be the actual life of God.' For them it may be 'a speaking image, a moving parable of divine life.' The temptation to claim that it is more leads some Christians to protest that it is less. It was as a hint of this that 'the primitive Christians, in the clumsy art of their catacombs, depicted Christ as Orpheus, the fabulous musician whose rhythm none could resist, who danced the fawns out of the forest and the firs down from the hill.'

To dismiss this as heathenism is to ignore the scriptural 'piped unto you, and ye did not dance' where people are recalled to a 'Jesus dancing them into the kingdom of God with the music of everlasting joy.' [3]

The element of reality which is behind primitive pagan dances has survived in the very different, because slowly measured and deliberately reverent, movements of the ministers at the Christian eucharist. The simplest and most austere version of the rite cannot but include this continuation of the ritual dance. For the eucharist is a thing done, and in order to do it the celebrant and assistants and communicants must move.

Actions are incorporated in the worship and bring into it bodily as well as mental and spiritual activities of the human

[3] Austin Farrer, 'David danced mightily' in *Said or Sung,* 1960, p. 185.

personality. But this has been so from the start. Christ could not have inaugurated it without performing actions : taking the bread and the wine, offering them, distributing them. Action in eucharistic worship is a necessary corollary from what Christ did.

A bridge between the ceremonial action in church and the moral service of a Christian in the world is the custom of processions. In many quarters of Christendom the procession forms part of any celebration of thanksgiving. It is associated with the major Christian festivals or other occasions when there is a special desire to return thanks, to give praise, to express spiritual joy. This spiritual act includes bodily action. All the themes of self-offering, self-sacrifice, dedication, can be gathered into it. It involves 'lips,' for a hymn is sung or a litany chanted as the procession moves : it involves 'lives,' for it is composed of people, ministers and choir who form a token body to represent the congregation if all do not personally take part in it. Most dramatic of all, the procession is an act of worship in which the worshippers are 'walking.' No petition could be more appropriate to the moment of a procession than that those who walk while they sing in church may sing in the world 'by giving up ourselves to thy service, and by walking before thee in holiness and righteousness all our days.'

Here the outward and visible and the inward and spiritual are closely knit. It is the characteristic feature of a sacramental religion. Lips are to strengthen lives, and lives can lead lips in the total offering of thankful and dedicated service.

Each element in the complete service of a Christian can support the other, but the working of divine inspiration alone can establish their unity in worship and life. Man cannot himself bring about the perfect unison of 'lips' with 'lives.' That is a further grace which comes in answer to the worshipper's prayer.

Strengthen for service, Lord, the hands
   That holy things have taken;
Let ears that now have heard thy songs
   To clamour never waken.

Lord, may the tongues which 'Holy' sang
   Keep free from all deceiving;
The eyes which saw thy love be bright,
   Thy blessèd hope perceiving.

The feet that tread thy holy courts
   From light do thou not banish;
The bodies by thy body fed
   With thy new life replenish.

Thus the early Liturgy of Malabar focused on the Eucharist
what was to be the final thought in *A general Thanksgiving*.

3

The scriptural call to praise embraces this employment of the
lips as an essential element without which man's offering to
God would be defective and incomplete. Lips according to
scripture are to be used in prayers and thanksgivings, even
when there is no desire to communicate the act of devotion
to other men or to share it with fellow-worshippers.

Scriptural writers consistently teach the offering of the lips
as a God-ward act, and this cardinal principle has been taken
from the ancient scriptures by the Church and woven into
the texture of her daily worship. Thus the recital or singing
of the daily offices of Morning and Evening Prayer always
includes the versicle and response from Psalm 51—

O Lord, open thou our lips
And our mouth shall shew forth thy praise.

The structure of the full version of anglican Mattins and Evensong emphasizes the prominence of this prayer for the opening of lips; for all that goes before is preliminary to this and is intended to lead on to the constant recognition that, whatever else may change in the ordered cycle of worship during the liturgical year with its varying moods and approaches, this one feature does not change. No corporate worship of any sort is to be offered, no complete witness in the daily life of the Christian is to be undertaken, without the inclusion in it of 'our lips.'

But this principle, evident and inevitable in Christian tradition, is one which modern worshippers have the greatest difficulty in observing. Our handicap is that we are for the most part prevented from preserving it in Christian worship because of our disposition to use lips, if at all, as means to an end. Whenever we deliberately allow our lips to open, we like to open them ourselves, and having avoided any request to God to open them we assume that our main purpose is communication with each other rather than with God. The test case occurs when we question whether we can naturally and without any form of self-consciousness use our lips when we are addressing God, not man. Nothing could be further from the thoughts or habits of most modern people. We find ourselves experiencing the opposite astonishment to that of Augustine (354–430) who, when he noticed Ambrose (*c.* 339–397) with a book, thought it an unusual thing that he was reading without moving his lips at all : 'When he was reading, his eye glided over the pages, and his heart searched out the sense, but his voice and tongue were at rest.' Augustine and his companions were so astonished by this behaviour that they were at a loss to account for it. All that Augustine himself could say was the generous remark that whatever Ambrose's purpose might be, 'certainly in such a man it was good.' [4] The episode marks a turning point in devotional manners. What was exceptional in Augustine's day is now the

[4] Augustine, *Confessions,* VI, 3.

rule. Few would now admit that use of the lips is necessary or even usual in private prayer or in study of the scriptures.

There are however indications that a change is taking place in the religious man's attitude to the service of our lips, and this is assisted by the development of certain aspects in contemporary life. The invention of the printing press and the consequent multiplication of printed books, magazines and papers have for some years got him into the habit of reading without the mouth. But he has read silently long enough.

> On all sides there is a revival of interest, and passionate interest, in the *heard* word, as distinct from the *written* word. Festivals, public readings, including radio broadcasts of verse, are attended with enthusiasm and critical appreciation. It is a sign of restored vitality, of a people beginning to realize the dangers resulting from cultural sloth, from the interference of outside ways of life (such as the Hollywood dictate), and from the folly of self-depreciation.[5]

Parallel with the use of comparatively recent mediums such as 'the tape-recorder, the long-playing gramophone record, the poetry broadcast or television programme' the younger poets expect their poems to be heard rather than read, and incline to the techniques of 'composition by breath-units, for the voice, not composition for the page.'[6]

What is of absorbing interest here is the new emphasis which this recovery is placing upon the voice as an expression of the total personality. When we are using our lips we are not using only our lips. The well-known bewilderment of the visitor at church who hears the choirboy's 'Prize 'im for 'is grice and fiver' next to a curate's 'Preeze him for his greece

---

[5] Richard Church, *Poems for Speaking*, 1950, p. 7.
[6] 'The British Imagination,' *Times Literary Supplement*, September 9th, 1960, p. xv.

and feever' is not merely caused by surprise that there should be different pronunciations of one language but by worry at the sort of personality behind one or the other. Equally understandable is a man's distaste for what used to be called the 'Oxford accent' or what is now recognizable as an artificial type of 'B.B.C. English,' in short, any affectation in speech, including 'the preaching of the Word of "Gud" to empty pews.' [7] People as well as pronunciations are involved, for humans are exercising their selves in the use of lips. This is well illustrated in the physical effort which has to be made by the man or woman who would use speech in public.[8] But the co-ordination of both mental and bodily factors in speech is not confined to public occasions, although then it is most noticeable. It is present in all speech, however private or intimate. By implication it is common to all forms of worship, including praise; and real praise from the lips will always be found to imply praise from the whole personality.

However, modern attempts to recover the solemnity of our lips tend to fail at one vital point. Throughout most of them the main interest remains fixed in communication. The spoken word is being addressed to men. Not that there is no hint whatever of a wider perspective. One literary critic, in describing 'the ultimate joy of reading aloud' as a 'memorable and happy experience' admits that from it 'the sense of communion lives on long after the book itself may have been almost forgotten.' [9] But here the communion, no less than the communication, is still between people, the reader and the listener, both human. The greater range of a Christian's spiritual experience offers the certainty to which these various efforts to restore speech are struggling, a communion with One greater than man, a mystic attachment of the soul and of the worshipping community to God. The Christian Church in the vocal use of her liturgy is demonstrating to our world

[7] Richard Church, op. cit., p. 5.
[8] See H. St. John Rumsey, *Clear Speech,* 1946, pp. 28–30.
[9] Oliver Edwards, *Talking of Books,* 1957, p. 22.

that there is a method of reading aloud which is not directed solely towards man, but is an employment of the lips yielding communion with God.

4

With these wider associations our concluding paragraph cannot be dismissed as a purely English example of so-called 'practical Christianity.' It is practical, for its bias is towards conduct; but it is also profound. How profound it is, appears as soon as it is seen in the setting, not merely of any particular trait or characteristic of our own national expressions of the Christian religion, but also of the main, central and energizing tradition of Christian spirituality.

The writer of the *General Thanksgiving* himself provides the clue which enables us to see how it belongs to this larger setting.

In the sermon which he preached to celebrate the escape of the city of London from the Plague and the Fire, Bishop Reynolds permitted himself to expand his views about unthankfulness. No doubt his lengthy and at times rhetorical treatment of his theme owed something to the feelings of the occasion; but extracts from his remarks will indicate the range of his view.

'Unthankfulness,' he claimed, 'is, not setting so high a price as we ought upon a good land, quiet habitations, fair estates, peaceable borders, flourishing fields, abundance of men, cattle, wealth, trade, strength, and other good things.' Next, he enumerates, 'unthankfulness for that which the apostle calleth "the riches of the world," and the "salvation of the Gentiles" (Rom. 11 : 11, 12); for the oracles of God, the ark of his presence, the glorious light of his gospel, and powerful means of grace and salvation.' Further, there is 'unthankfulness (which is worse) in abusing mercies, waxing fat by them, and then kicking against the author of them; filling ourselves in our pastures, and then forgetting God; . . . turning peace into security, and plenty into excess, and grace into lasciviousness, and pardoning mercy into presumption of sinning.' Finally, 'the not using a mercy, is to be unthankful for it : how much more sad account must men give of abused mercies? of requiting the goodness of the Lord with forsaking of him; the culture and husbandry, the rain and dew which he hath bestowed upon them, with thorns and briars (Deut. 32 : 6; Luke 13 : 7; Heb. 6 : 7). As the greater heat of the sun doth more speedily ripen fruit, so do great mercies hasten the maturity of sin.' [10]

In all this the preacher was making clear that there is more in unthankfulness than ingratitude, just as there is more in thanksgiving than simple gratefulness. The unthankfulness which he was describing was in fact the reason for the repetitions—his own term is 'ingeminations'—of the word 'praise' (not thanks) in the psalms. 'In the last psalm, containing but six verses, we are called upon thirteen times to praise the Lord. Jewels are made of divers precious stones couched together : praise is a jewel, a comely, a beautiful thing (Ps. 33 : 1); and we find one of these jewels is made up of no fewer than six and twenty ingeminations (Ps. 136).'

Reynolds takes this thought as his cue for what may be counted as one of the finest descriptions of what praise is, based upon the two phrases 'Praise him for his greatness, he is the Lord' and 'Praise him for his goodness, he is thy God.'

If a man shew me a precious and stately thing, I shall be thankful out of curiosity, as for a favour; but if he shew it, and then give it, I shall be a thousand times thankful, as for a rare bounty. Great and good, and *mine*: nothing will move thankfulness, if excellency and property will not. The greatness of his power mine to keep me; the greatness of his wisdom mine to counsel me; the greatness of his grace mine to sanctify me; the greatness of his glory mine to save me;—who should be thankful, if not they who want

[10] *Works,* Vol. V, pp. 15–16.

nothing? And who can be said to want any thing who have God for their God? 'The Lord,' said David, 'is my shepherd : I shall not want' (Ps. 23).[11]

The author of our *Thanksgiving* writes in this way about the nature of praise and the psalmist's repeated calls to praise in order to draw attention to man's proneness to unthankfulness. In doing so he sketches in the details of what unthankfulness is. It is 'not setting so high a price as we ought' on blessings or possessions. It is 'not using a mercy.' It is 'abusing mercies.' In short, the opposite to thanksgiving and its kindred praise is not only the not saying 'Thank you.' It implies a condition of the soul of which this not-saying is but one symptom.

5

The masters of the spiritual life agree that the opposite to thankfulness is more than the absence of it. Neither unthankfulness, nor lack of gratitude, nor even selfishness is adequate to describe it. Rather it is dullness of soul, spiritual dryness, an emptiness, malaise, listlessness. It shows itself in various symptoms : grumbling, sullenness, complaining, fretting, prolonged restlessness. These are the signs, whether or not the condition is accompanied by bitterness and envy against both God and neighbour. The condition has acquired the name of 'accidie.'

We possess an outline sketch of this condition, which 'we may describe as tedium or perturbation of heart,' in the writings of John Cassian of Marseilles (*c.* 360–435).

When this besieges the unhappy mind, it begets aversion from the place, boredom with one's cell, and scorn and contempt for one's brethren, whether they be dwelling with one or some way off, as careless and unspiritually minded persons. Also, within the enclosure of our own lair, we

[11] *Works,* Vol. V, p. 15.

become listless and inert. It will not suffer us to stay in our cell, or to attend to our reading : we lament that in all this while, living in the same spot, we have made no progress, we sigh and complain that bereft of sympathetic fellow-ship we have no spiritual fruit; and bewail ourselves as empty of all spiritual profit, abiding vacant and useless in this place ; and we that could guide others and be of value to multitudes have edified no man, enriched no man with our precept and example. . . . Finally one gazes anxiously here and there, and sighs that no brother of any description is to be seen approaching : one is for ever in and out of one's cell, gazing at the sun as though it were tarrying to its setting : one's mind is in an irrational confusion, like the earth befogged in mist : one is slothful and vacant in every spiritual activity, and no remedy, it seems, can be found for this state of siege than a visit from some brother, or the solace of sleep. Finally our malady suggests that in com-mon courtesy one should salute the brethren, and visit the sick, near or far. . . .[12]

This description of the 'malady born of the spirit of accidie' is couched in terms which apply to the life of a monk. Only slight adaptation is required to make it fit the circumstances of any person in the world.

It is significant that Cassian gives as the cure for this spiritual illness the directions of St. Paul : 'Study to be quiet, and to do your own business, and to work with your own hands, as is commanded you' (1 Thess. 4 : 11). He makes no mention of self-training in thankfulness or of practising thanksgiving or of 'counting one's blessings,' which has no less support from the Epistles and might be advanced as the remedy by a less profound adviser. The cure for moroseness or dejection in the life of a Christian is not to be found in our lips, but in our lives. It is not provided by what we say, no matter how correct that be, no matter how loaded it be

[12] H. Waddell, *The Desert Fathers*, 1936, pp. 157–8.

with formal and proper thanksgivings. It is provided by action according to one's vocation, by the thankfulness which is expressed in attending to one's 'own business' of living one's life according to the divine will and of studying 'to be quiet' in fulfilling the purpose of God.

Cassian's account became the source for much elaboration of the theme during later centuries. Its spirit is vividly embodied in the implications of the 'practical' conclusion to our *Thanksgiving*.

Next we may notice a remarkable parallel which is provided by the practice of Meditation or Mental Prayer. A feature of this form of prayer [13] is that it occupies a fixed period of time : fifteen minutes or half an hour or more, according to the rule or capacity of the individual. During this period attention is given to a theme or 'mystery' of the faith or to some episode or verse taken from scripture, especially from the gospels. It may be done individually or in a group.

What is the place of thanksgiving in such prayer? An answer is indicated by two of the more widely used methods of Mental Prayer : the Salesian, named after François de Sales (1567–1622), who expounded it in his classic of the devotional life, *An Introduction to the Devout Life,* and the Method of Peter of Alcantara (1499–1562), described by him in his *Treatise on Prayer and Meditation.*

F. P. Harton [14] analysed the two methods as follows :

1. *Scheme of the Salesian Method*

    (i) *The Preparation*
        (a) Recollection of the Presence of God
        (b) The Invocation
        (c) The setting forth of the Mystery

[13] For a full account see, for example, W. L. Knox, *Meditation and Mental Prayer,* and Bede Frost, *The Art of Mental Prayer.*
[14] F. P. Harton, *The Elements of the Spiritual Life,* 1932, pp. 243–9.

(ii) *The Considerations*

(iii) *The Affections and Resolutions*

(iv) *The Conclusion*
 (a) Act of Thanksgiving
 (b) Act of Oblation
 (c) Act of Petition
 (d) The Spiritual Nosegay

2. *Scheme of the Method of Peter of Alcantara*

(i) *Preparation*
 (a) Act of Recollection
 (b) Act of Contrition
 (c) Invocation of the Holy Spirit

(ii) *Reading*

(iii) *Meditation*
 (a) Imaginative
 (b) Intellectual

(iv) *Thanksgiving*

(v) *Offering*
 (a) Of self
 (b) Of the merits of Christ

(vi) *Petition*
 (a) Intercession
 (b) Petition
 (c) Prayer for the love of God.

In both these schemes the portion of time allotted to Thanksgiving comes in the middle. The period of Mental Prayer is not to end with thanksgiving, but with intercession, petition or offering, or, as in the vivid suggestion made by François de Sales, in the gathering of a spiritual nosegay of thoughts or themes which is done in the manner of one, who, about to leave a friend's garden, takes away a few choice blooms.

In following either scheme we omit neither adoration nor thanksgiving. But these acts come early in the course of the complete act of meditation, so that when the period of prayer is over we do not return to the world with an abrupt finish to our acts of love for God, but with a quiet resolution and readiness to carry the will of God into the world. The soul quietens down before re-entering the daily round of duty or of trial.

The conclusion to our *Thanksgiving* (which is nearly contemporary with both Methods) copies this order with astonishing exactness. The transference of thought from 'lips' to 'lives' and the insistence upon 'walking before thee in holiness and righteousness all our days' are a replica of the conclusion to both these standard Methods of Meditation.

Further, the similarity in the ending is part of a remarkable parallelism which obtains throughout the prayer. The two schemes which are outlined above show a common tendency to follow a given sequence : Preparation—including recollection of the presence of God ; Meditation—including Adoration and Thanksgiving ; Conclusion—including Petition and Offering. *A general Thanksgiving* falls quite naturally into those three main sections.

1. 'Almighty God, Father of all mercies . . .' includes the Recollection with Adoration and Praise ;
2. 'We bless thee for . . .' invites Meditation and leads on to renewed Adoration and to spoken Thanksgiving ;
3. 'And, we beseech thee, give us that due sense . . .' marks the conclusion which includes both Petition and an act of self-offering.

In short, the *Thanksgiving* itself can be taken as a frame for

H

these Methods of Meditation. It can be offered by individuals slowly and meditatively, clause by clause, as a Method of Mental Prayer. Its corporate use, which is the more usual, obscures this fact. But the corporate use does not exclude this other way of praying it. No less than the Lord's Prayer or the Creed or the Gloria, or indeed any other form of traditional worship, the *General Thanksgiving* can be used as an extended exercise of private devotion. It is then that its inner structure is revealed as closely corresponding to the schemes of Mental Prayer which are already familiar to Christians for that purpose.

In taking into account the traditional Christian conception of the nature of 'accidie' and the developments in the methods of Mental Prayer we have looked far beyond the borders of anglican devotion, and we have seen enough to be able to assert that our *Thanksgiving* and, in particular, its conclusion are in harmony with the deeper tones of Christian spirituality

Not only can we claim that the final paragraph in our prayer suits the human temperament and condition by reintroducing the worshipper quietly and firmly to the lower levels of life in the world, but also we have grounds for recognizing in this prayer the outlines of authentic Christian devotion. In it is preserved for the benefit of all who use the Book of Common Prayer a short guide to the kind of devotion which Christians have shared throughout the main traditions; for in learning this prayer the worshipper is accepting that genuine rhythm of the soul's life which moves deliberately and serenely from thanksgiving to dedication, from the sanctuary to the world.

This is the movement described by Evelyn Underhill as spiritually going downstairs, a movement which has to continue until we can say that 'we have got to the bottom of the stairs now and are fairly sitting on the mat.' [15] It is the sequence which is exemplified in Paul's order of the fruit of

[15] E. Underhill, *The Fruits of the Spirit*, 1942, p. 36.

as in the New English Bible, 'harvest' of the Spirit which opens with the attractive trio, 'love, joy, peace,' but reaches a climax in the less colourful 'fidelity, gentleness and self-control' (N.E.B.); or in the pattern of the Lord's Prayer which leads us from contemplation of the splendour of the Father's Name, Kingdom and Will to the pedestrian human concerns of bread, trespasses, dangers. We find nothing forbidding, nor even frustrating, in this direction of our souls as long as we see in it the path of him who by his incarnation 'came down to earth from heaven.' Christ's own descent is the route for the Christian's self-humbling in the dedicated life. That cannot cancel thanksgiving, praise and adoration; rather it completes them.

The Prayer Book provides two other outstanding examples of this movement. The prayer of thanksgiving at the close of the Communion Service has this ending, based on Ephesians 2 : 10 : 'And we most humbly beseech thee, O heavenly Father, so to assist us with thy grace, that we may continue in that holy fellowship, and do all such good works as thou hast prepared for us to walk in'; and the Collect for the Second Sunday after Easter—closely allied to our *General Thanksgiving,* as we have noted, by its use of the adjective 'inestimable'—not only prays that 'we may always most thankfully receive' the 'inestimable benefit' of Christ's sacrifice for sins, but also that we may endeavour to follow 'the blessed steps of his most holy life.' In both these examples the intimate interrelation between Christian thankfulness and the Christian life is clearly stated. The theme is integral to acceptance of the Christian gospel. There is no need for the conclusion to our *Thanksgiving* to act as an anti-climax in the Christian's experience. His return to this world is to display the reality of his thanks and to prepare him for his own renewal of thankfulness when next he comes to repeat the prayer.

Scripture supplies much of the wording for *A general Thanks-giving*. Individual phrases recall scriptural associations. Well-known words belong to scriptural contexts. Even the one significant term in the *Thanksgiving* which does not appear in the Authorized Version—'inestimable'—is charged, as we have seen, with biblical ideas. But by far the most weighty quotation from the Bible comes at the end of the concluding petition for grace to live a thankful life. Bishop Reynolds found it in St. Luke.

The extent and importance of this quotation may be judged by comparing the two passages.

Luke 1 : 74–5 gives

That he would grant unto us, that we . . . might serve him without fear, in holiness and righteousness before him, all the days of our life.

Our *General Thanksgiving* has

Give us that due sense of all thy mercies, that . . . we shew forth thy praise . . . in our lives; by giving up ourselves to thy service, and by walking before thee in holiness and righteousness all our days.

The author of our prayer has skilfully adapted his quotation. 'All the days of our life,' for example, becomes 'all our days' and so conforms to the required rhythm of the clause; this is in contrast to the use of the phrase, unaltered, in the Prayer for the Church Militant. But the use of 'service,' 'before thee,' 'holiness and righteousness' makes the quotation unmistakable. What Reynolds has done is to take this passage from Luke and expand it sufficiently to adapt it to his own purpose without obscuring its origin.

Righteousness and holiness are mentioned together in two

other passages in the New Testament. Ephesians 4 : 24 has : 'That ye put on the new man, which after God is created in righteousness and true holiness.' Romans 6 : 19 reads : 'even so now yield your members servants to righteousness unto holiness.' The association of these two texts with Luke 1 : 75 helped to formulate the interpretation which was current when our *Thanksgiving* was composed.

Matthew Henry's exegesis on the verse in Luke may be taken as typical of the time. According to him *holiness and righteousness* form a pair which 'includes the whole duty of man towards God and our neighbour.' Further, to serve, or in the words of our prayer to walk, *before him,* means

> to serve him, *before him* in the duties of his immediate *worship,* wherein we present ourselves *before the Lord,* to serve him as those that have an eye always upon him, and see his eye always upon us, upon our inward man, that is serving him, *before* him ;

and 'all the days of our life' or 'all our days' is to imply that

> the design of the gospel is to encourage us to constancy and perseverance in the service of God, by showing us how much depends upon our not drawing back, and by showing us how Christ *loved us to the end,* and thereby engaged us to *love him to the end.*

Meditation upon these extracts throws up points of contact with other scriptural themes and contexts, all of them finding a focus in the text from Luke.

The phrase 'in holiness and righteousness' lasted as far as the Revised Standard Version. The New English Bible substitutes 'with a holy worship, with uprighteousness of heart.' But the passing of time has not been able to divorce the two linked words when either is employed in a balanced survey or practice of religion. 'These two words,' a modern commentator writes, 'represent the two sides of religion, Godward and manward.' He adds : 'the perfect religion is that which holds the right balance between the two, allowing neither to out-weigh the other.' We have examples of excessive emphasis upon asceticism, austerity, self-discipline in some Eastern forms of the Christian and other religions. At the opposite extreme it is a common feature of religions in the West to draw attention in an emphatic manner to the ethical demands of 'practical religion.' But

> each of these is insufficient by itself. Holiness without Righteousness becomes egocentric and selfish, while Righteousness without Holiness can degenerate into a godless, man-made substitute for true religion.[16]

The two words which are used together in the canticle of Zachariah have thus become inseparable in the estimate of those who would follow a mature form of Christianity. The Prayer Book has taken them from the New Testament and has preserved them together in the Prayer for the Whole State of Christ's Church, in the Litany, and in the third Exhortation provided in the Communion Service. But their most impressive use in worship is that which comes in the course of our *Thanksgiving;* here they are repeated as a direct quotation from the original Gospel verses.

What will most invigorate the Christian as he reaches this end to his thanksgiving will be his recognition not merely of its verbal parallels with the Bible but of the scriptural setting from which it is taken.

The quotation with which Bishop Reynolds has chosen to close the prayer is from the song of Zachariah, our *Benedictus.* This is a song of new births and new beginnings. Occasioned by the birth of the Fore-runner it celebrates in anticipation the birth of the Saviour. It is inseparable from the narratives of the Nativity. It is an anthem of a nascent religion, of a

[16] J. H. R. Moorman, *The Path to Glory,* 1960, pp. 16–17.

Christianity still in its own infancy and rejoining in a Saviour's infancy, and of a Church which remains the young or 'early Church.' This is the song which has become a morning canticle. Each day that it is repeated it respeaks the mood of births and beginnings, and it witnesses to a perennial youthfulness at the heart of Christian faith, a signal that the Church of this or any later century is still the early church, summoning every soul to continue living in the morning of discipleship. No Christian can faithfully rehearse this song without in some respect starting his Christian life afresh. It will not allow us to forget that we remain 'little children' even if we get beyond the threshold of the kingdom.

In this mood the quotation brings to a close our *Thanksgiving*. It is a mood which requires to be recognized, investigated and willingly encouraged if it is not to be lost, and it forms a crowning conclusion to a prayer of thankfulness. Too often man's sincerest expressions of thanks look only to the past. We thank God for blessings which have already been received. We thank him for mercies which have already been granted. We join with the universal church in offering praise for a redemption which, being historical, is dated in the past. But this final act in *A general Thanksgiving* bids us supplement that view by turning round and looking for the dawning of a new Day. Before him who is the Eternal we are to serve and to walk 'all our days.' Only to him can we give thanks and service for the future and eternity; for to him belong

ALL HONOUR AND GLORY,

WORLD WITHOUT END,

AMEN